The World-Directedness of Emotional Feeling

"In this carefully researched book, Müller offers detailed and sustained criticisms of standard accounts of emotional experience or feeling as a kind of 'axiological receptivity'—a form of taking in how the world is evaluatively. Müller argues that such accounts fail properly to make sense of the intentionality and the phenomenology of emotions. In its place, he proposes an original 'position-taking' account of emotional experience that understands it to be the taking of a positive or negative stand towards significant objects, and he argues that this better accounts for the intentionality and phenomenology of emotions, as well as the sense in which emotions are deeply personal.

The sustained criticisms Müller offers of standard accounts of emotional feeling should be taken seriously, and Müller's positive account is rich and interesting on its own: an important and distinctive contender, with wide-ranging implications for philosophy of mind quite broadly. *The World-Directedness of Emotional Feeling* amply repays the time invested in reading it."
—Bennett Helm, *Franklin & Marshall College, Pennsylvania, USA*

"Concerning the widely discussed idea of the specific intentionality of emotions, Müller provides an original and convincing account. Partly following the work of Peter Goldie, who famously introduced the term of 'feeling towards', Müller argues in the tradition of analytical philosophy, at the same time drawing on the tradition of early phenomenologists of the beginning of the 20th century. Rigorous, clear and accurate, this is a very fruitful endeavour."
—Eva Weber-Guskar, *Guest Professor of Philosophy, Humboldt University of Berlin, Germany*

Jean Moritz Müller

The World-Directedness of Emotional Feeling

On Affect and Intentionality

Jean Moritz Müller
University of Bonn
Bonn, Germany

ISBN 978-3-030-23819-3   ISBN 978-3-030-23820-9 (eBook)
https://doi.org/10.1007/978-3-030-23820-9

© The Editor(s) (if applicable) and The Author(s), under exclusive license to Springer Nature Switzerland AG, part of Springer Nature 2019
This work is subject to copyright. All rights are solely and exclusively licensed by the Publisher, whether the whole or part of the material is concerned, specifically the rights of translation, reprinting, reuse of illustrations, recitation, broadcasting, reproduction on microfilms or in any other physical way, and transmission or information storage and retrieval, electronic adaptation, computer software, or by similar or dissimilar methodology now known or hereafter developed.
The use of general descriptive names, registered names, trademarks, service marks, etc. in this publication does not imply, even in the absence of a specific statement, that such names are exempt from the relevant protective laws and regulations and therefore free for general use.
The publisher, the authors and the editors are safe to assume that the advice and information in this book are believed to be true and accurate at the date of publication. Neither the publisher nor the authors or the editors give a warranty, expressed or implied, with respect to the material contained herein or for any errors or omissions that may have been made. The publisher remains neutral with regard to jurisdictional claims in published maps and institutional affiliations.

Cover illustration: © Melisa Hasan

This Palgrave Pivot imprint is published by the registered company Springer Nature Switzerland AG
The registered company address is: Gewerbestrasse 11, 6330 Cham, Switzerland

I used to know someone quite self-absorbed and stubborn who spent lots of time and energy telling himself it was utter hubris to try and finish what ultimately became this slim book. It is, of course, up to the reader to judge whether it has anything to offer worth pondering. But please forgive my self-indulgence if I feel that, in light of my disputes with this person, I owe it to him to correct him: it's finished.

Acknowledgements

This book grew out of my research at the University of Manchester, which I completed in July 2014. My deepest gratitude goes to my Doktorvater Joel Smith, whose feedback has been invaluable in developing the central ideas of this work. I could not have hoped for more support—and patience—along the way. Besides Joel, many others have provided crucial impulses and insightful advice. It is thanks to Jan Slaby that I got interested in the emotions in the first place and am grateful to him for his excellent comments on earlier versions of some of this material. In coming to terms with the ideas discussed in this book and developing my own angle on the matter, I have hugely benefitted from conversations with Martin Cajthaml, Julien Deonna, Sabine Döring, Gregor Hochstetter, Kevin Mulligan, Michelle Montague, Alba Montez Sanchez, Hichem Naar, Achim Stephan, Fabrice Teroni and Íngrid Vendrell Ferran. I would also like to thank Catharine Abell, Sean Crawford, Michael Clarke, Philip Letts, and Michael O'Sullivan for their written comments on previous drafts of some of the chapters, as well as Julian Dodd and Bennett Helm for their extensive feedback on the first complete draft.

Some this work draws on and develops material taken from my article "Emotion as Position-Taking" (*Philosophia* 46(3), 525–540).

I would like to thank the editor of *Philosophia*, Asa Kasher, as well as Springer Nature for their kind permission to reuse this material. I am indebted also to my editor at Palgrave-Macmillan, Lauriane Piette, for her kind support throughout the publication process. Work on the core material for this book was ultimately possible due to a grant I received for my Ph.D. studies from the Arts and Humanities Research Council, UK, which I hereby gratefully acknowledge.

Writing a book-length essay (even if it's ultimately a slim volume) can be quite taxing. For the courage and stamina to push on and bring the project to a close, I owe special thanks to Dave Harris, who has offered lots of kind and insightful advice on how to best approach the task of writing a dissertation and getting it published, too. For their wonderful support throughout various stages of the dissertation process, I moreover owe deep thanks to Fiamma Rupp-Gembs, Jan Friedeborn, Gözde Naiboglou, my former colleagues at PhinisheD, as well as my parents. Sadly, my father passed away before the book got published, but he witnessed the completion of my dissertation, which I would like to think of as by far the most significant step on the way to the published book. I am incredibly grateful also to my dear partner, Juliana Kohl, for her support with my decision to publish my dissertation, for the many hours spent on helping to correct the index of the book, as well as for making sure that, whilst preparing the manuscript, I devoted enough time to those sides of life that philosophy simply cannot compensate for.

I owe special thanks to Peter Goldie, who supervised my Ph.D. until his unexpected death in October 2011. Peter's own work on emotion and his philosophical outlook—especially regarding the importance of being accurate to ordinary experience—have significantly influenced my research. I hope that Peter would have been sympathetic to my take on his notion of "feeling towards" in this book.

It goes without saying that any flaws and oddities that have remained in the text despite the enormous help I received are solely my own fault. Last but not least, I owe an apology to those philosophers who have developed views on emotional feeling and intentionality, which I came across only in the late stages of preparing the manuscript and have not been able to discuss in the text. Especially, I would like to apologize to Jonathan Mitchell, whose work on this topic I hope to be able to engage with in future work.

Contents

1	**Introduction**	1
	1 The Significance of Emotional Feeling	2
	2 Feeling, 'Cognizance-Taking' and 'Position-Taking'	5
	3 Overview of Individual Chapters	11
	References	13
2	**Feelings and Formal Objects**	17
	1 The Felt Aspect of Emotion	18
	1.1 Jamesian Sensations	20
	1.2 Hedonic Tones	27
	2 Formal Objects	36
	2.1 The Significance of Formal Objects	38
	2.2 Axiological Realism	42
	3 Conclusion	45
	References	46
3	**Emotional Feeling as Receptivity to Value**	51
	1 The Manifest Image of Emotion According to the Axiological Receptivity View	54

    2 How the Axiological Receptivity View Fails the Manifest Image of Emotion: Feeling Towards 58
    3 Feeling Towards and Responsiveness 63
    4 A Possible Concern: Affectivity and Directedness 75
    5 Implications for the Significance and Structure of Formal Objects 78
    6 Conclusion 82
    References 84

4 Emotional Feeling as Position-Taking 89
    1 The Idea 90
    2 Substantiating the Notion of Emotional Position-Taking 97
        2.1 The Personal Dimension of Hedonic Tone 101
        2.2 Hedonic Tone as Position-Taking 105
    3 Emotional Feeling as Position-Taking and as Evaluative Attitude 107
    4 Conclusion 109
    References 111

5 The Evaluative Foundation of Emotional Feeling 113
    1 Feeling Value 116
    2 Concern-Based Construals as Receptivity to Value 119
    3 Construals and Conceptual Capacities 127
    4 How to Think of Construals as a Form of Epistemic Access 132
    5 Conclusion 140
    References 141

6 Conclusion 145

Index 149

1

Introduction

Abstract Emotions are significant to us in part in virtue of involving feeling. Moreover, on a currently widely held view, their significance derives from the fact that the feeling involved in emotions is inseparable from their world-directed aspect or intentionality. On this view—which I call *intentionalism*—, how we feel in being afraid of some object or event is inextricably intertwined with the way we are psychologically involved with this object or event. In this opening chapter, I introduce intentionalism and specify the main aim of this book. As the view is usually elaborated, emotional feelings constitute a form of perception-like apprehension of axiological properties or values. I call this the *axiological receptivity view* (AR). My goal is to show that AR is mistaken and to propose and defend a more adequate intentionalist account of emotional feeling.

Keywords Emotional feeling · *Gemütsbewegung* (stirring of the sensitive mind) · Intentionality · Axiological receptivity · Perception of value · Position-taking

1 The Significance of Emotional Feeling

It is central to our ordinary conception of emotions that these have a felt or phenomenal dimension. Emotions are often described as stirrings of the soul or, more evocatively, as stirrings of the *sensitive mind* (cf. the German term "*Gemütsbewegung*"[1]). In thus describing them we allude to a characteristic type of felt agitation, a certain felt inner movement, which is central to the way we experience them. This felt aspect also appears to be what we have in mind in calling them "affective". The term "affect", if taken literally, similarly alludes to a characteristic sense of inner movement—a sense of being touched or affected—that seems integral to emotional phenomenology. Such descriptions are, of course, generic. Considerations on the phenomenology of emotion suggest that emotions typically involve feelings which are characterized by a subtlety that is sometimes thought ineffable, yet is often surprisingly well expressed in literary narratives:

> His melancholy, which was settling into a secondary stage, like a healing wound, had in it a certain acrid, palatable sweetness. (James 2013 [1877], 320)

> I felt so keen a longing for Mme Guermantes that I could scarcely breathe; it was as though part of my breast had been cut out by a skilled anatomist and replaced by an equal part of immaterial suffering, by its equivalent in nostalgia and love. And however neatly the wound may have been stitched together one lives rather uncomfortably when regret for the loss of another person is substituted for one's entrails; it seems to be occupying more room than they; one feels it perpetually; and besides, what a contradiction in terms to be obliged to *think* a part of one's body. (Proust 1996 [1920–1921], 131)

In line with many philosophers, past and present, I will here assume that an adequate view of emotions ought to recognize them as having a specific

---

[1]The term "*Gemüt*" is notoriously hard to translate. "Soul" is one common choice. It does not capture all the relevant connotations, however, which is why I opt for "sensitive mind". Cf. Scheer (2014) for a very illuminating overview of the history of the term.

felt aspect.[2] Accordingly, I am concerned with emotion qua conscious episode or occurrence. To deny that emotion involves a characteristic, often complex and subtle, felt inner agitation—to deny that emotions are affective—is to ignore what we would commonly recognize as their most essential and salient dimension.[3] Relatedly, it would seem to severely impoverish our conception of the significance of emotions in our lives. That emotions matter to us, it seems, is in large part due to their affective character, to the often complex and subtle ways we feel in having them. Emotions make a distinctive contribution to our mental lives *qua feeling*.

In the philosophical literature on emotion, we find various different attempts to illuminate emotional feeling in ways that are sensitive to the significance we pre-theoretically ascribe to it. While I take it that most theorists who attempt to do so would accept the generic description I have given so far, not everyone agrees on how emotional feeling ought to be characterized in detail and what precisely its role in our psychological lives comes down to. If we survey the views that have emerged over the past few decades, it seems, however, that there is a notable consensus that an account of emotional feeling that is sensitive to its intuitive significance must reject what has traditionally been thought of as a strict conceptual dichotomy. As many have come to believe, in order to properly appreciate emotional feeling as an important aspect of our psychological lives we must not think of it as mere feeling, as the exemplification of purely phenomenal properties or *qualia*. Rather, we ought to conceive of it as exemplifying that feature of our minds which is arguably responsible for the fact that the emotions found their way back into analytic philosophy in the first place: as a bearer of *intentionality*.

---

[2] One might wonder whether there are emotions that lack any felt aspect. Cf. e.g. Roberts (2003, 2013). It seems to me that philosophers who assume so ultimately confuse emotions with the disposition to have them. Cf. Döring (2009, 14, n. 4). In this connection, cf. also Deonna and Teroni (2012, chapter 1). I here adopt what I take to be the most common view, on which there is always something it feels like to have an emotion.

[3] About half a century ago, when the emotions were rediscovered by analytic philosophers, feeling was sometimes thought irrelevant to understanding emotion. Cf. e.g. Bedford (1957), Kenny (2003 [1963]), Pitcher (1965). It seems to me that, in most cases, this attitude was, at least in part, an artifact of a rather simplistic conception of feeling, which was insensitive to any of the above alluded complexities.

Stated in general, non-technical terms, the principal intuition guiding these philosophers is that the felt aspect of emotion constitutes a certain type of *psychological involvement with the world*. As they propose, we render emotional feeling intelligible as making an important contribution to our mental lives by recognizing it as a specific way in which our mind is 'directed upon' features of our present situation or in which such features are 'given' to our mind. Not everyone agrees on how precisely to characterize the specific way in which we are psychologically involved with the world in emotional feeling. But there seems to be growing agreement that emotional feelings (at least in part) owe their significance to the fact that they constitute a form of intentionality.

It is important to stress that the view in question—which I will refer to as *intentionalism* about emotional feeling—is a view specifically of the *felt aspect* of emotion. Since their renaissance as a research topic in Anglo-American philosophy in the 1950s and 1960s, emotions have been widely recognized as intentional. Thus, it has been widely noted that emotions take objects, that we are afraid *of* people, angry *at* them or glad *that* they share our concerns.[4] And much of the philosophical research on emotion since then has largely revolved around the topic of intentionality. However, in line with the standardly assumed divide between intentionality and phenomenal consciousness in philosophy of mind at the time, it was long common to suppose that in recognizing emotions as intentional one is concerned with an aspect *distinct* from their felt dimension. Emotions were widely conceived as *compound occurrences* that comprise both an intentional act or state and a separate, non-intentional feeling component (e.g. Neu 1977, 161; Thalberg 1977, 32; Lazarus et al. 1980, esp. 192 and 198; Lyons 1980, 81; Calhoun 1984; Gordon 1987). Intentionalism about the felt aspect of emotion can be seen to be, in part, a reaction against this traditional picture.[5] As many suppose, in denying

---

[4] To be more precise, one might also put this point by saying that emotions have *particular objects* or *targets*. The particular object or target of an emotion is the object which is picked out by the noun or propositional complement of the psychological verb by means of which it is canonically ascribed. I say more about the notion of a target in Sects. 2 and 3 in Chapter 3.

[5] Some theorists who think of the felt aspect of emotion as intentional still embrace a compound view, according to which an emotion comprises further intentional acts or states in addition to feeling. Cf. e.g. Goldie (2000, chapter 1; 2002, 2009). What is rejected in this case is not the idea that emotions are compound occurrences but the claim that their felt dimension is non-intentional.

intentionality to emotional feelings themselves this picture leaves us with a seriously impoverished conception of them and of the emotions more generally, a conception that is bound to ignore the distinctive place of affectivity in our mental lives.[6]

I agree with this outlook and believe that the feeling/intentionality dichotomy that characterizes traditional philosophical theorizing about the emotions is misguided. That is, I share the intuition that emotional feeling constitutes a specific way of being psychologically involved with the world as well as the belief that it makes a significant contribution to our mental lives in virtue of being intentional. While sympathetic to the broader outlook that characterizes large parts of the more recent debate on occurrent emotion, I yet also believe that there is a widespread confusion on the precise shape a satisfactory intentionalist view of emotional feeling should take. More precisely, I believe that the most commonly offered account in this context is crucially inadequate with respect to the intentional features and, accordingly, the kind of significance it accords to the felt dimension of emotion. Hence, I take it that there is considerable philosophical work to do in reorienting the debate towards a more adequate account of the place of emotional feeling in our mental lives.

In the remainder of this introduction, I set out the more specific dialectical thread of this book. In the following section, I introduce what I take to be the main intentionalist view of emotional feeling in the contemporary debate and specify more precisely how I intend to reorient and contribute to this debate. I then provide an outline of the book's more specific argumentative structure.

2 Feeling, 'Cognizance-Taking' and 'Position-Taking'

"How can a mere *feeling* constitute an experience in which the world reveals itself to us?" asks John McDowell (1998 [1983], 130) towards the

---

[6] It is fair to say that perhaps not everyone who rejects the feeling/intentionality divide does so with a view to illuminating the idea that emotional feeling plays a significant role in our psychological lives. But it seems to me that many philosophers who reject this divide do. It is theorists with this specific aim that I refer to as intentionalists about emotional feeling.

end of an intricate discussion of a central problem in the philosophy of aesthetic value. If we survey the more recent literature on emotion, it seems that many contemporary philosophers do not share the skeptical attitude to which this question gives voice.[7] There is a surprisingly unified agreement that the felt aspect of an emotion is an experience of just this kind: emotional feelings apprehend genuine aspects of the world; they are presentations of value. Roughly, the idea is that, in favourable circumstances, the feelings involved in emotions like joy and disappointment disclose a certain object or event as having positive or negative value, respectively (e.g. Weberman 1996; Tappolet 2000, chapter 6; Helm 2001, esp. chapter 2; 2002, 2009; Roberts 2003, 2013, chapter 3; Zagzebski 2003; Döring 2004, chapters 8 and 9; Ammann 2007, esp. chapter 2.2; Slaby 2008, esp. chapter 9; Deonna and Teroni 2008, 79ff., Poellner 2016).[8]

According to the view propounded by these theorists—which I shall call the *axiological receptivity view* (for short: AR)—, the recognition of emotional feeling as a distinctive type of intentional occurrence coincides with its recognition as significant. Emotional feeling is thought to make a crucial contribution to our mental lives *qua intentional*. In being conceived as presentations or impressions of value, emotional feelings are understood as playing a specific *epistemic* role: as axiological presentations their job is to make us aware of value by *acquainting us with* value.[9]

---

[7] It is worth highlighting that McDowell himself is not party to this skepticism.
[8] These authors hold this view in different degrees of strength. My reading of Tappolet (2000, chapter 6) as a proponent of this view is largely based on her remarks on Goldie's notion of 'feeling towards' in her review of Goldie (2000). Cf. Tappolet (2002). Poellner (2016) advocates a qualified version of this view, which holds for a restricted class of emotion. There are also views on which emotion is assimilated to perception while it is not (or not explicitly) supposed that the role of presenting value is played specifically by their felt aspect. Cf. e.g. Pelser (2014). Also, some authors draw analogies between emotion and perception without supposing that emotions present values, but argue, for example, that both reliably co-vary with values. Cf. e.g. Cuneo (2006). In this connection cf. also Brady (2013, chapter 2), Dokic and Lemaire (2013). Note further that, unlike McDowell, none of the philosophers I have mentioned are concerned specifically with *aesthetic* value.
[9] From now on, I use the term "value" to refer to both positive value and negative value (disvalue).
    According to some proponents of AR, the importance of emotional feeling resides mainly in a specific justificatory role. That is, some suppose that qua affective acquaintance with value emotions provide a specific type of warrant for corresponding evaluative judgments. Cf. e.g. Tappolet (2000, chapter 7), Döring (2004, chapters 8 and 9), Roberts (2013, chapter 3). The claim that emotions justify evaluative judgments has also been defended independently of AR, e.g. by arguing that emotions and perceptions both serve as evidence for certain states of affairs, as Cuneo (2006) has it.

The reasons for which AR is found compelling by many theorists differ to some extent. However, many seem to be attracted to the view in large part inasmuch as they suppose that it is an accurate rendition of the manifest image of emotion. As they suppose, ordinary experience represents the felt inner agitation characteristic of emotion as a form of value impression. On the view of emotional phenomenology assumed by them, emotional feeling constitutes a way in which value or significance is 'given to' or made manifest to us in something like the way sensory properties are apprehended in ordinary sense-perceptual experience.

It is perhaps also not hard to see why AR may seem compelling as an alternative to traditional views of emotional feeling that presuppose a divide between feeling and intentionality. In the case of sensory receptivity, i.e. ordinary sense-perceptual experience, intentional mode and phenomenal consciousness seem inextricably intertwined. In having a visual experience of the redness of a cherry, say, the presentation of colour seems inseparable from *what it is like* to enjoy this experience, its phenomenal character. The notion of presentation points to a rather natural way of making sense of the idea that the intentional features of mental occurrences may coincide with their phenomenal character.

Although AR may seem attractive in several respects, it seems to me that this view is fundamentally flawed. The central aim of this book will be to show that AR seriously misrepresents the role we ordinarily recognize emotional feeling as playing in our psychological lives and that it therefore ought to be abandoned in favour of a different intentionalist view. In my assessment of AR, I will not be guided by common meta-ethical concerns regarding the possibility of a perceptual or quasi-perceptual access to value. I will rather show that the view is in strong tension with what it (partly) purports to explicate, i.e. the manifest image of emotion. As should become evident in the first half of the book, properly elucidated, our ordinary conception of emotion clearly distinguishes emotional feeling from presentation. As they feature in ordinary experience and discourse, emotional feelings constitute a type of intentional occurrence that is in a certain sense the exact opposite of presentations or impressions.

In this connection, cf. also Brady (2013, chapters 2.3 and 2.4). In this work, I will not, or at least not explicitly, be concerned with the justification of evaluative judgment.

In offering this criticism, I simultaneously pave the way for an alternative intentionalist view. As I go on to show, this view recognizes it as making a radically different contribution to our mental lives.

According to the view I set against AR, emotional feeling is *directed towards* the world in a specific way that makes it intelligible as *responsive to* value. In this respect, it crucially contrasts with ways of registering—or being receptive to—value. On this conception, the felt agitation characteristic of emotion is *based on* the apprehension of value, rather than being constitutive of it. Giving a more substantial description, we can say that emotional feeling constitutes a certain type of *position-taking* (*Stellungnahme, prise de position*).[10] In feeling angry, sad or disappointed, we do not come to be acquainted with or 'take cognizance' (*Kenntnis nehmen*) of the disvalue of something; rather we take a certain negative position towards it because of its disvalue. Similarly, in feeling glad, proud or enthusiastic, we do not apprehend positive value, but rather take a positive stand towards something in light of its positive value. More specifically, I shall propose that the significance of emotional feeling resides in large part in the fact that it constitutes the taking of a positive or negative position on some object or event in response to its value, where this position is crucially informed by our personal investments, that is, by our *cares and concerns*.

The picture I propose—which I shall call the *position-taking view* (PT)—is not entirely new. It looms large in the German early realist phenomenological tradition, in particular in the writings of Dietrich von Hildebrand (1969a [1916], 1969b [1922], 1953). I will draw in part on von Hildebrand's phenomenological considerations in criticizing the account of emotional feeling offered by AR and introducing PT as an alternative. I will ultimately go on to develop the view in considerably more detail, however, and spell out at some length what precisely makes it apt to think of emotional feelings as position-takings.

Although there is a strong trend towards an understanding of emotional feeling as fundamentally epistemic, the main intuition I will set against AR is also shared by at least a few theorists in the contemporary debate.

---

[10] I here opt for a direct English translation of the German and French locutions. Some authors use the terms "attitude" (e.g. Mulligan 2004, 217; 2007, 210) or "stance" (e.g. Salice 2016) instead. As I explain in Sect. 1 in Chapter 4, these locutions seem less fortunate to me in this context.

For example, Nussbaum (2001) can be seen as holding a similar position. If carefully read, she can be understood as proposing that the felt agitation of emotion is a distinctive type of intellectual position-taking, a form of intellectual assent to the way things axiologically appear (e.g. ibid., 45). However, Nussbaum's view differs considerably from the one I defend. In particular, Nussbaum offers a reductive account of emotional feeling, which assimilates it to intellectual occurrences. In contrast to her, I follow von Hildebrand in understanding it as a *sui generis* form of position-taking.[11]

A contemporary view that essentially corresponds to the one I will defend can instead be attributed to Mulligan (esp. 2007, 2010a, b). Mulligan understands emotion as a sui generis position-taking which is responsive to value. Moreover, though this is not explicit, one might read him as defending this view more specifically with respect to their felt aspect.[12] Mulligan likewise explicitly advocates his position in opposition to an understanding of emotion as receptivity to value. At the same time, he does not go very far in explicating and defending the basic intuition underlying PT. In particular, he does not say very much about what precisely makes emotional feelings position-takings.[13]

As I have emphasized, my concern in this investigation is explicitly with the felt dimension of emotion and thus with what is usually conceived as a *specific aspect* of them. While this is not central to my main explicative aim, we will see, as a collateral result, that there are reasons to suppose that the distinction between emotional feeling and (occurrent) emotion is ultimately empty. As the discussion proceeds, emotional feeling will become intelligible as possessing just those features philosophers have traditionally

---

[11]Although sympathetic to AR, Helm (2001, 45f., 64ff.) and, following him, Slaby (2008, 242f.), might be seen to espouse a closely related account which avoids reductionism. They partly conceive of emotional feeling as a type of distinctive, non-intellectual assent to value. However, this view differs from the one I propose as well in how it conceives of the intentionality of emotional feeling. Cf. Sect. 1 in Chapter 4, p. 90.

[12]In his (2010b) Mulligan distinguishes between the affective aspect of emotion and its cognitive base. He can plausibly be read as defending the view that emotions are position-takings with respect to their affective aspect. In this connection, cf. also my remarks on Mulligan's view in Sect. 1 in Chapter 4.

[13]I mention some further cognate views in Chapter 4. I there also explicitly compare my proposal with a recent view by Deonna and Teroni (2012, chapter 7; 2014, 2015) that has recently been receiving considerable attention and can seem to be based on the same core intuition.

attributed to emotions, but often relegated to a dimension separate from their felt aspect. These centrally include their intentional features, their intimate link to cognition and their conditions of appropriateness or fittingness. While I sympathize with many theorists in the contemporary debate on emotion who take this to be sufficient to identify emotion and emotional feeling,[14] I shall however ultimately remain neutral on this question. As far as I can see, most of my central considerations are compatible also with accounts of emotion that recognize occurrent emotions as comprising intentional feelings amongst other psychological constituents.

Before I move on to detailing the precise structure of this investigation, I would like to add one final comment on my methodological commitments. As will already have transpired, my central concern is with the manifest image of emotion. I am concerned to provide an adequate philosophical account of the nature and significance of emotional feelings as they feature in common, everyday experience. Accordingly, my arguments will be primarily based on the way emotional feelings present themselves from a first-person point of view—their phenomenology—and the linguistic and conceptual structures we deploy in ascribing and making sense of them. While the account I wish to provide is principally informed by our pre-theoretical notion of emotion, I will at the same time consider and respond to certain philosophical concerns that arise in connection with some of its metaphysical and epistemological commitments. Thus, part of my discussion will also be aimed at defending or vindicating, rather than just explicating, certain aspects of our ordinary conception of emotion.

In choosing this approach, I do not mean to propose that common sense or our ordinary conception of emotion are the ultimate arbiters of the success of any philosophical investigation into emotional feeling. My belief is rather that an explication of the manifest image of emotion contributes a kind of understanding that is both unique and important and therefore deserves careful attention in its own right. The approach I choose might be called broadly hermeneutic insofar as it aims at a better understanding of

---

[14] The view proposed by these theorists is not to be confused with the traditional feeling theory of emotion, commonly associated with James (1884, 1891) and, sometimes, Hume (1978 [1738–1740], bk. 2). According to the latter, emotional feelings are identical to non-intentional sensations. The present proposal might be considered a more sophisticated feeling theory which dispenses with the dichotomy between feeling and intentionality.

ourselves and our way of living. This type of understanding is an understanding from within those very practices it is ultimately concerned to illuminate, rather than an understanding from the 'objectifying' point of view of an independent, uninvolved observer. In this respect, it contrasts with the type of understanding sought by theorists with a more empirically minded approach. While I recognize that there may be different views as to the merits of the approach I adopt, I hope that the considerations in the chapters to follow demonstrate that studying emotional feelings from this angle—as an aspect of our way of living—is both interesting and worthwhile.

3   Overview of Individual Chapters

In Chapter 2, I elaborate on the generic description of emotional feeling I have provided at the outset and introduce two further assumptions regarding emotion and value that will prove useful in discussing AR and explicating the alternative picture I favour. In the first, main part of the chapter, I reject the common view that emotional feeling is a type of bodily sensation and argue that a closer look at our description of emotions as stirrings of the sensitive mind supports an altogether different view. I shall argue that emotional feeling is a form of psychological (dis)comfort (hedonic tone) that possesses a characteristic personal dimension and defend this picture against a number of objections. In the second part, I explicate the widely held idea that emotions are correlated with a specific type of value property which plays an essential role in determining their intelligibility, fittingness and individuation conditions: their *formal objects*. In this context, I also briefly discuss a specific metaphysical commitment that is implied by recognizing emotions as subject to fittingness conditions determined by their formal objects, i.e. a commitment to axiological realism. This chapter prepares the ground for the main dialectical thread.

The third chapter initially introduces in some more detail the common phenomenological motivation for AR, which is further precisified as the view that the felt aspect of an emotion is a presentation of the corresponding formal object. I then show AR to drastically misrepresent the way emotional feelings feature in ordinary experience. As I argue, an adequate view of their phenomenology represents emotional feelings as an intentional mode that fundamentally differs from impressions or presentations, a mode which I shall call, following Goldie (2000, chapters 2 and 3; 2002, 2009), 'feeling towards'. As I argue, feeling towards is a specific form of psychological involvement with the particular object of an emotion which contrasts with presentation in virtue of how it is directed toward this object. The relevant difference can be further explicated by noting that feeling towards is a *response* to certain aspects of its object. I further expand on my criticism of AR by showing that, understood as feeling towards, emotional feeling is necessarily responsive in particular to *value* and can therefore not be conceived as apprehending value since it already presupposes awareness of it. I conclude this chapter by rejecting AR.

In Chapter 4, I offer PT as an alternative to AR. As I propose, in recognizing the felt aspect of emotion as feeling towards we simultaneously recognize it as a specific kind of position-taking and thus as occupying a rather different place in our psychological lives. I first introduce the basic idea of this alternative picture and then go on to elaborate it so as to make it intelligible as offering a substantial rather than mere metaphorical account of emotional feeling. I do so by offering a more thorough account of the kind of (dis)comfort constitutive of emotional feeling, which shows it to be intimately related to our cares and concerns. I also contrast the view with a recent account of emotions and their felt aspects, which is defended by Deonna and Teroni (2012, chapter 7; 2014, 2015) and can initially seem very similar to PT.

The fifth chapter further lays out PT by offering a more thorough account of the axiological awareness on which emotional feelings are based as responses to value. While expanding on PT by clarifying the nature of this awareness, it also aims at responding to a common worry about the possibility of value awareness. In this chapter, I disperse this worry by proposing a candidate for an evaluative foundation of emotional feeling that can be recognized as an instance of a familiar, non-mysterious class of mental phenomena. My response should also help remove an obstacle to accepting the realist view of the formal objects of emotions that is implied by their role in determining fittingness conditions for emotions, since this worry is often invoked in support of a skeptical attitude against value realism.

Perhaps the main concern of this investigation will seem fairly specific. It is basically concerned with two different ways of understanding the idea that emotional feeling occupies a specific role in our mental lives insofar as it possesses intentionality. However, it would be wrong to suppose that what is at stake here are merely two variants of one and the same basic conception of the significance of emotional feeling. As should become apparent in the chapters to follow, it makes a tremendous difference how we choose to explicate this idea.

References

Ammann, Christoph. 2007. *Emotionen*. Stuttgart: Kohlhammer.
Bedford, Errol. 1957. Emotions. *Proceedings of the Aristotelian Society* 57: 281–304.
Brady, Michael. 2013. *Emotional insight*. Oxford: Oxford University Press.
Calhoun, Cheshire. 1984. Cognitive emotions? In *What is an emotion?*, ed. Cheshire Calhoun and Robert Solomon, 236–247. New York: Oxford University Press.
Cuneo, Terence. 2006. Signs of value: Reid on the evidential role of feelings in moral judgment. *British Journal for the History of Philosophy* 41 (1): 69–91.
Deonna, Julien, and Fabrice Teroni. 2008. *Qu'est-ce qu'une émotion?* Paris: Vrin.
Deonna, Julien, and Fabrice Teroni. 2012. *The emotions*. London: Routledge.
Deonna, Julien, and Fabrice Teroni. 2014. In what sense are emotions evaluations? In *Emotion and value*, ed. Sabine Roeser and Cain Todd, 15–31. Oxford: Oxford University Press.
Deonna, Julien, and Fabrice Teroni. 2015. Emotions as attitudes. *Dialectica* 69 (3): 293–311.
Dokic, Jerôme an Stéphane Lemaire. 2013. Are emotions perceptions of value? *Canadian Journal of Philosophy* 43 (2): 227–247.
Döring, Sabine. 2004. *Gründe und Gefühle*. Habilitationsschrift [Second book]. Duisburg-Essen University.
Döring, Sabine. 2009. Allgemeine Einleitung: Philosophie der Gefühle heute. In *Philosophie der Gefühle*, ed. Sabine Döring, 12–65. Frankfurt am Main: Suhrkamp.

Goldie, Peter. 2000. *The emotions*. Oxford: Clarendon Press.
Goldie, Peter. 2002. Emotion, feeling and intentionality. *Phenomenology and the Cognitive Sciences* 1 (3): 235–254.
Goldie, Peter. 2009. Getting feelings into emotional experience in the right way. *Emotion Review* 1 (3): 232–239.
Gordon, Robert. 1987. *The structure of emotions*. Cambridge: Cambridge University Press.
Helm, Bennett. 2001. *Emotional reason*. Cambridge: Cambridge University Press.
Helm, Bennett. 2002. Felt evaluations: A theory of pleasure and pain. *American Philosophical Quarterly* 39 (1): 13–30.
Helm, Bennett. 2009. Emotions as evaluative feelings. *Emotion Review* 1 (3): 248–255.
Hume, David. 1978. *A treatise of human nature*, ed. Lewis A. Selby Bigge. Oxford: Clarendon Press. Original edition: 1738–1740.
James, Henry. 2013. *The American*. London: Sovereign (1st ed. 1877).
James, William. 1884. What is an emotion? *Mind* 9: 188–205.
James, William. 1891. *The principles of psychology*, vol. 2. London: Macmillan.
Kenny, Anthony. 2003. *Action, emotion and will*. 2nd ed. London: Routledge and Kegan Paul (Original edition, 1963).
Lazarus, Richard, Allen D. Kanner, and Susan Folkman. 1980. Emotions: A cognitive-phenomenological analysis. In *Emotion*, ed. Robert Plutchik and Henry Kellerman, 189–217. New York: Academic Press.
Lyons, William. 1980. *Emotion*. Cambridge: Cambridge University Press.
McDowell, J. 1998. Aesthetic value, objectivity, and the fabric of the world. In *Mind, value and reality*, 112–130. Cambridge, MA: Harvard University Press. Original edition: McDowell, John. 1983. Aesthetic value, objectivity, and the fabric of the world. In *Pleasure, preference and value*, ed. Eva Schaper, 1–16. Cambridge: Cambridge University Press.
Mulligan, Kevin. 2004. Husserl on the "logics" of valuing, values and norms. In *Fenomenologia della ragion pratica*, ed. Beatrice Centi and Gianna Gigliotti, 177–225. Naples: Bibliopolis.
Mulligan, Kevin. 2007. Intentionality, knowledge and formal objects. *Disputatio* 23 (2): 205–228.
Mulligan, Kevin. 2010a. Husserls Herz. In *Husserl und die Philosophie des Geistes*, ed. Manfred Frank and Niels Weidtmann, 209–238. Berlin: Suhrkamp.
Mulligan, Kevin. 2010b. Emotions and values. In *Oxford handbook of the philosophy of emotion*, ed. Peter Goldie, 475–500. Oxford: Oxford University Press.

Neu, Jerome. 1977. *Emotion, thought and therapy*. London: Routledge and Kegan Paul.
Nussbaum, Martha. 2001. *Upheavals of thought*. Cambridge: Cambridge University Press.
Pelser, Adam. 2014. Emotion, evaluative perception, and epistemic justification. In *Emotion and value*, ed. Sabine Roeser and Cain Todd, 107–123. Oxford: Oxford University Press.
Pitcher, George. 1965. Emotion. *Mind* 74: 326–346.
Poellner, Peter. 2016. Phenomenology and the perceptual model of emotion. *Proceedings of the Aristotelian Society* 116 (3): 261–288.
Proust, Marcel. 1996. *In Search of Lost Time. Vol. 3: The Guermantes Way*, trans. C.K. Scott Moncrieff and T. Kilmartin, rev. D. J. Enright. London: Vintage. Original edition: Proust, Marcel. 1920–1921. *Le côté de Guermantes*. Paris: Gallimard.
Roberts, Robert C. 2003. *Emotions*. Cambridge: Cambridge University Press.
Roberts, Robert C. 2013. *Emotions in the moral life*. Cambridge: Cambridge University Press.
Salice, Alessandro. 2016. The phenomenology of the Göttingen and Munich circles. In *Stanford encyclopedia of philosophy* (Winter edition), ed. Edward Zalta. http://plato.stanford.edu/entries/phenomenology-mg/. Accessed 1 April 2019.
Scheer, Monique. 2014. Topographies of emotion. In *Emotional lexicons: Continuity and change in the vocabulary of feelings 1700–2000*, ed. Ute Frevert, Monique Scheer, Anne Schmidt, Pascal Eitler, Bettina Hitzer, Nina Verheyen, Benno Gammerl, Christian Bailey, and Magrit Pernau, 32–61. Oxford: Oxford University Press.
Slaby, Jan. 2008. *Gefühl und Weltbezug*. Paderborn: Mentis.
Tappolet, Christine. 2000. *Émotions et valeurs*. Paris: Presses Universitaires France.
Tappolet, Christine. 2002. Long-term emotions and emotional experiences in the explanation of actions: A critical review of Peter Goldie's *The emotion: A philosophical exploration*. In *European review of philosophy 5: Emotion and action*, ed. Elisabeth Pacherie, 151–161. Stanford: CSLI Publications.
Thalberg, Irvin. 1977. *Perception, emotion and action*. Oxford: Basil Blackwell.
von Hildebrand, Dietrich. 1953. *Christian ethics*. New York: McKay.
von Hildebrand, Dietrich. 1969a. *Die Idee der sittlichen Handlung*. Special Edition. Darmstadt: Wissenschaftliche Buchgesellschaft. Original edition: von Hildebrand, Dietrich. 1916. Die Idee der sittlichen Handlung. Jahrbuch für Philosophie und phänomenologische Forschung 3: 126–251.

von Hildebrand, Dietrich. 1969b. *Sittlichkeit und ethische Werterkenntnis.* Special Edition. Darmstadt: Wissenschaftliche Buchgesellschaft. Original edition: von Hildebrand, Dietrich. 1922. Sittlichkeit und ethische Werterkenntnis. Jahrbuch für Philosophie und phänomenologische Forschung 5: 463–602.
Weberman, David. 1996. Heidegger and the disclosive character of the emotions. *The Southern Journal of Philosophy* 34 (3): 379–410.
Zagzebski, Linda. 2003. Emotion and moral judgment. *Philosophy and Phenomenological Research* 66 (1): 104–124.

2

Feelings and Formal Objects

Abstract This aim of this chapter is to prepare the ground for the main argument of the book. In the first part, I elaborate on the nature of emotional feeling by examining the common characterization of emotions as affective or, alternatively, as stirrings of the sensitive mind (*Gemütsbewegung*). I reject the popular view that emotional feeling is a type of bodily sensation and argue that it is instead a form of psychological (dis)comfort (hedonic tone) that possesses a characteristic personal dimension. In the second part, I explicate the widely held view that emotions are correlated with a specific type of value property which plays an essential role in determining their intelligibility, fittingness and individuation conditions: their *formal objects*. Against this background, I precisify the axiological receptivity view (AR) and the intentionalist alternative I intend to develop, which are both interpreted as relating emotional feelings to their formal object.

Keywords Bodily sensation · Hedonic tone · Formal object · Axiological realism

I have introduced the claim that emotions possess a specific felt dimension in terms of the notion of a characteristic felt inner movement or agitation. I take this description to be warranted on pre-theoretical grounds. However, it is not very precise. Before I discuss in more detail the currently predominant intentionalist view of emotional feeling, I want to first elaborate on this notion and specify more clearly what type of feeling I take emotions to comprise. This is what I set out to do in the first section of this chapter.

In order to help focus the discussion in one further respect, I shall moreover introduce a concept that allows us to precisify the formulation of the two rivalling intentionalist views I will be concerned with. Contemporary philosophers of emotion recognize emotions as being intimately related to specific value properties. There is a wide consensus that each emotion type is correlated with one particular value or disvalue—its *formal object*. As I understand them, the view that emotional feeling is receptivity to value (AR) and the view that it is a position-taking (PT) both conceive of the felt aspect of an emotion as bearing a specific link to its formal object. In Sect. 2 of this chapter, I explicate the notion of the formal object of an emotion and briefly address one implicit commitment of views that ascribe formal objects to emotions—axiological realism.

1 The Felt Aspect of Emotion

Let me begin with a brief comment on how I introduced the idea of emotional feeling. I noted two ways in which occurrent emotions are ordinarily described—as stirrings of the soul or sensitive mind (*Gemütsbewegungen*) and as affective. Both allude to a characteristic felt inner movement or agitation that gives some content to the claim that they possess a specific felt aspect.

Without wanting to enter into intricate phenomenological details right at the beginning, I would like to briefly acknowledge and respond to a potential worry with this initial account. As I claimed, our use of the term "affective" in this context refers to a certain sense of being touched or affected, which is integral to ordinary emotional experience. I take this claim to resonate closely with the phenomenology of mental occurrences we regard as paradigmatically emotional, such as fear, anger, joy, sadness, indignation, pride, admiration, remorse, jealousy and shame. However, while most philosophers would presumably agree that these occurrences involve a characteristic felt inner agitation, some might find fault with the claim that they involve a sense of being affected. Thus, some philosophers distinguish between occurrent emotion and a phenomenon they call "being affected".[1] The phenomenon of being affected comprises experiences such as being offended by someone's insult or being enchanted by a work of art, which are to be distinguished from emotional occurrences such as being angry at an offender or admiring a work of art. In describing emotions as involving a certain sense of being affected, they might object, I am illicitly assimilating two distinct types of experience and thereby miss out something distinctive to the type of felt agitation characteristic of genuine emotional experience.

While I agree that there are some differences between mental occurrences such as being offended or enchanted and occurrent anger or admiration, including differences regarding the way we feel in having them, I would maintain that both types of occurrence are phenomenally similar in an essential respect. That is, both essentially involve a felt inner movement or stirring of the same basic kind, as is evidenced by our referring to both as stirrings of the sensitive mind (*Gemütsbewegungen*). Moreover, I would insist that this type of agitation is aptly described in both cases in terms of being touched or affected. There is good reason why we classify paradigm emotions as affective. I thus take this concern to be ill-founded in that it ignores a fundamental phenomenal similarity.[2]

---

[1] Though he does not use the terms "emotion" and "feeling" or "felt aspect", I take this to be a possible reading of von Hildebrand's (1953) position. Cf. esp. (ibid., 207ff., 317ff). On being affected cf. also von Hildebrand's taxonomy in (2007 [1965], chapter 2) and my remarks in Müller (2019, section 1). Mulligan (2007) similarly seems to draw a distinction between emotions and affects. What Mulligan says in other places (2009, 155) makes it less clear that he sees a sharp distinction here.

[2] One might wonder whether this similarity provides sufficient reason to class both types of occurrence as emotion proper. In this connection cf. also Cova and Deonna (2014). I believe that there are also certain phenomenological differences, which provide some warrant for distinguishing the two. However, showing this would require me to enter into several subtleties which would lead us too far afield. In this work, I will be focusing exclusively on the felt aspect of phenomena we ordinarily recognize as paradigm emotions.

Supposing that my initial account of emotion as comprising a characteristic felt inner agitation or sense of being affected is accurate, let us then ask how this felt dimension can be characterized in more detail. What precisely does the affectivity of emotion involve?

1.1 Jamesian Sensations

Even a very cursory look through many twentieth century publications in Anglophone philosophy of emotion suggests that the default view for many philosophers is that emotional feeling is essentially bodily, that is, a specific type of proprioceptive awareness. On this conception, the affective dimension of emotion essentially consists in awareness of peripheral bodily reactions. That is to say that emotional feeling is conceived as an experience of a specific constellation of physiological changes.

This view is commonly associated with William James' feeling theory of emotion (James 1884, 1891),[3] but it is found also in a great number of places in the literature that has emerged in the second half of the twentieth century. Somewhat precisifying this view, we can say that most of its recent proponents propose that the sensations in question amount to an awareness of the following types of physiological occurrence: changes in the striated muscles involved in movement and posture, changes in facial and vocal expression, as well as changes of the visceral nervous system (e.g. heart rate, perspiration, respiration) and the endocrine system (e.g. adrenaline). To feel afraid, angry, glad, or sad, they claim, is to register changes along some or all of these dimensions. I shall here refer to these sensations as *Jamesian sensations*.

To many, this view of emotional feeling possesses considerable plausibility insofar as such felt bodily changes are usually present in occurrences of many paradigm emotions. Thus, in fear or anger, for example, one often experiences sensations of muscular tension, of accelerated breathing and heart rate and, at least in the former case, of a rush of adrenaline.

---

[3] James' view is proposed as a view of occurrent emotion, rather than of its felt aspect in particular. However, in identifying emotions with a specific type of bodily sensation, he ultimately takes emotions to be identical with their felt aspects.

This view can also seem plausible in that such changes capture a genuine sense of inner agitation or movement.

That said, while popular, there are various respects in which one might find fault with the Jamesian view of emotional feeling. For example, considering the literature on James' feeling theory, one finds several considerations which are primarily targeted against the identification of emotion with Jamesian sensations, but can also be brought to bear against an understanding specifically of its felt aspect in somatosensory terms. As far as I can see, there are at least three criticisms that need mention.

One perhaps rather obvious point is that there are emotional occurrences which do not obviously have a proprioceptive feel (cf. Nussbaum 2001, 60; Poellner 2016, 272f.). Consider, for example, occurrences of pride, admiration, awe, nostalgia, pity or regret. Though these may be accompanied by bodily sensation, this need not and often is not the case.[4] Still, it seems that in these cases, too, there is a felt aspect. Also, bodily sensations are not obviously always present in the case of emotions that are usually accompanied by them (cf. Nussbaum 2001, 60f.; Deonna and Teroni 2012, 65). For example, even fear and anger may occur in such weak forms that it is hard to tell whether they involve awareness of any bodily changes of the above specified types. Still, all of these emotional occurrences involve feeling.

According to a further criticism, the view is falsified by the observation that there is a certain phenomenal uniformity to our sense of being affected across occurrences of a given type of emotion. There is *a* characteristic feeling or felt dimension of fear (feeling afraid) and, likewise, *a* characteristic feeling or felt aspect of anger (feeling angry), of sadness (feeling sad), of joy (feeling joyful) etc. which phenomenally unifies occurrences of the respective type of emotion.[5] The Jamesian sensations that accompany occurrences of a given emotion type however often seem to vary considerably. Thus, it is not clear that the same set of sensations is present across different occurrences of fear or anger (cf. Nussbaum 2001, 61).

---

[4] Poellner takes this to be true also of indignation. Nussbaum's counter-example is grief.

[5] Nussbaum may not agree with this (cf. ibid., 61ff.), though I think it is a fairly natural view. Note, also, that I do not mean to deny, that there is no variation at all to our sense of being affected across occurrences of a given emotion type. Cf. also Sect. 2 in Chapter 1.

The view thus seems unable to accommodate what is phenomenally common to individual occurrences of a given emotion type.

Finally, the proposal may seem to be contradicted by a pathological case. There is empirical evidence in support of the claim that patients with spinal cord lesion still enjoy emotional feelings even though they seem to lack awareness of peripheral bodily responses. Early, much discussed investigations on spinal cord injuries by Cannon (1927, 1929) suggest that impaired peripheral physiology does not lead to reduced occurrent emotion. The issue has been investigated also with a particular focus on the experiential dimension of emotion in a more recent study by Cobos and collaborators (2002), whose findings suggest that spinal cord lesions do not diminish emotional feeling.

These objections seem well taken. It may not be obvious that they are sufficient to discard the view, however. Thus, in response to the first criticism, proponents of the proposal might insist that more careful introspection reveals emotional occurrences which do not obviously involve a proprioceptive feel to still be accompanied by at least some, albeit minor, felt visceral agitation after all. This may perhaps strike one as a blunt move, but it does not seem completely outré to maintain that many of the alleged counter-examples are ultimately harder to adjudicate than it initially seems and to thus try and question their dialectical bearing.

Likewise, there are responses to the latter two criticisms. Thus, the third and perhaps prima facie most severe one might be answered by appeal to a prominent empirical proposal by Damasio and his collaborators (2000; cf. also Prinz 2004, 58f.; Deonna and Teroni 2012, 65). This proposal provides some evidence for the view that, whist lacking awareness of physiological changes of the relevant sort, patients with spinal cord lesions still enjoy awareness *as of* such changes. That is, it points to a possible qualification of the Jamesian view that accommodates these cases by conceiving of emotional feelings as generally identical with proprioceptive registerings as of particular bodily changes, which may but need not constitute genuine registerings of such changes.[6]

---

[6]At least one study on spinal cord lesions seems to have produced findings in line with the Jamesian view of emotional feeling. Thus, Hohmann (1966) reported that his patients did have reduced emotional experiences. These findings have not been replicated, though. Cf. also Cobos et al. (2002) for discussion.

Finally, proponents of the view might further insist that we can also recognize some phenomenal uniformity to the bodily sensations that are present across occurrences of a given emotion type if we pay close enough attention to the way they present themselves in ordinary experience. According to one such proposal, offered by Deonna and Teroni, the various sensations that accompany an emotion are always experienced as playing a unified psychological role, which is invariant across occurrences of a given emotion type (e.g. 2008, 79f.; 2012, 79ff.; 2014, 2015). This role is characterized (in part) as that of preparing the body for action.[7] Thus, the bodily sensations present in fear are thought to jointly constitute a felt bodily action readiness for flight or attack, which is stable or uniform across individual occurrences of fear. Deonna and Teroni in fact add a further dimension to this psychological role which resonates closely with the main concern of this investigation: the felt action readiness constituted by Jamesian sensations is taken to ultimately apprehend a particular value property, e.g. danger in the case of fear. They can be read as proposing that the sensations that accompany individual occurrences of fear are phenomenally uniform across such occurrences in that they are always experienced as playing a specific epistemic role.[8]

In light of these responses, it may thus seem that there is some room to manoeuver for proponents of a Jamesian view in handling the above objections. Yet, while one might thus doubt that they are very damaging to the view, it would be wrong to conclude that the Jamesian account is a serious candidate for a more precise characterization of emotional affectivity. This is because there is a further, more important reason to be skeptical about it. Considering the generic account of emotional feeling I initially provided more carefully, it seems that the appeal to awareness as of muscular, autonomic and endocrine changes provides a rather misleading

---

[7] Deonna and Teroni here draw on a proposal that looms large in certain areas of empirical psychology. Cf. esp. Frijda (1986, 2007) on the idea that emotions are action tendencies. A prominent precursor to Frijda's position is Arnold (1960a, b).

[8] This claim is central to their position in (2008). It still forms part of their more recent 'attitudinal view' of emotion (2012, chapter 7; 2014, 2015). Cf. esp. (2014, 16) on the intuition that emotions apprehend value. As I read their (2012, chapter 7), they suppose that the felt aspect of an emotion 'makes manifest' evaluative aspects of the situation. Admittedly, this reading may be controversial in the case of their (2015), though in this article they also do not explicitly distance themselves from this view. I return to Deonna and Teroni's attitudinal view in Sect. 3 in Chapter 4.

picture of the characteristic felt agitation of emotion. As they feature in ordinary experience and discourse, occurrent emotions present themselves as involving feelings of a very different sort.⁹

In referring to emotions as stirrings of the sensitive mind (*Gemütsbewegungen*), we allude to a felt agitation which, on the face of it, lacks any proprioceptive dimension (or, at any rate, proprioception in the common, somatosensory sense elucidated above). It possesses a qualitative character that is entirely missing in sensations of muscular, visceral and endocrine changes. In locating this felt agitation in the soul or sensitive mind, we seem to highlight this distinctive qualitative character. Borrowing Stocker's (1996, chapter 1) terms, we might say that emotional feeling is *psychic* rather than proprioceptive.¹⁰ The relevant experiential difference is emphasized also by Descartes (1931 [1649]). As he proposes, the feelings involved in emotion are felt "as though they were in the soul itself" (1931 [1649], I.25; cited in Stocker 1996, 19) and are thereby to be distinguished from bodily sensations, which "we relate to our body or some of its parts" and "perceive as though they were in our members" (both quotes from ibid, I.24; cited in Stocker 1996: 19). The notion of a bodily sensation in play in Descartes' discussion of the emotions may be considerably simpler than the one that has been elaborated in connection with James' feeling theory. Yet Descartes' phenomenological account captures an intuition that seems to me no less pertinent on a modern Jamesian view of bodily sensations. The naïve phenomenology of emotion suggests that it possesses a felt dimension that is altogether different from experiences

---

⁹ I also think that there are problems for the above response to the problem of phenomenal uniformity insofar as it conceives of emotional feeling as apprehending value. These will become apparent in Chapter 3.

¹⁰ The term "psychic" is also used by Scheler (1973 [1913–1916], 342) to characterize certain emotions (especially certain forms of sadness and joy). Cf. also Mulligan (2008, 597), Vendrell Ferran (2008, 151f.), and Poellner (2016, 237). Stocker's use of the term is broader in that it refers to the felt aspect of emotion in general. Moreover, Scheler might be read as according a felt bodily dimension to psychic emotions (cf. also Vendrell Ferran 2008, 152). This felt bodily dimension (what is often called "*leibliches Spüren*"—the feeling of the 'lived body') is different from bodily sensations, though. While there is much to say about views that link emotional feeling to this felt bodily dimension, the topic of the 'lived body' is a world of its own, which I will here have to set aside. Cf. Vendrell Ferran (2008, chapter 5), Slaby (2008, chapter 13) for helpful attempts at relating these views to the contemporary Anglophone debate on emotion.

as of changes in our internal physiological landscape, a felt dimension that occupies a rather different 'phenomenological location'.[11]

The inadequacy of a Jamesian construal of emotional feeling becomes apparent also if we consider more closely what is implied by our ordinary description of emotions as affective. We thereby seem not to refer to a mere physiological arousal or affectation. Rather it is *we*—as subjects with certain cares and concerns—that are palpably moved or touched. To think of emotions as affective is to ascribe to them a sense of being *personally* affected: to feel afraid is to be affected as someone who *is attached to* something (e.g. one's bodily, mental or social integrity), to feel angry is to be touched as someone who *upholds* and *is invested into* certain norms or standards. This intuition is not captured by a view of emotional feeling as essentially physiological. To think of affectivity in terms of sensations as of muscular, autonomic and endocrine perturbations is to ignore its distinctively personal dimension. As I understand this idea of a personal dimension, it further precisifies the specific qualitative character alluded to by referring to emotions as stirrings of the sensitive mind. That is, rather than referring to a different aspect of the phenomenology of occurrent emotion, this idea offers a possible take on the claim that emotional feelings are located in the sensitive mind: it is their intimate link to specific aspects of our personhood—our cares and concerns—which accounts for the impression that they are, phenomenologically speaking, differently situated than bodily sensations.

It might be thought that the intuition I am looking to impart here depends upon an understanding of Jamesian sensations as purely physi-

---

[11] On the notion of phenomenological location in this context, cf. Rosenthal (1983, 184). I owe this point to Whiting (2012, 100, n. 100). The experiential difference I am after specifically concerns emotional feeling in comparison to Jamesian sensations. I do not mean to deny that there are any experiences that both have a bodily phenomenology and also involve *Gemütsbewegungen*. For a striking example, consider the comparison proposed by Helm (2001, 93f.) between the pleasant sensation of a lover's caress, the painful sensation of a rapist's caress (given with identical gentleness) and the hedonically neutral sensation enjoyed when accidentally brushing by the velvet drapes. While there is clearly a somatically locatable feeling in all three cases, one might think that, in the first and second, the experience cannot be completely assigned to a particular bodily location. To be fair, the (un)pleasantness of the respective experience seems to be primarily 'centred' around the touched surface of subject's arm. As the rapist strokes the victim's arm, it is that part of her body which 'hurts'. At the same time, I would like to think that this (dis)pleasure is also in part derivative of a certain background agitation that does not seem to have a clear somatic location. This latter felt agitation does not seem to be proprioceptive.

ological occurrences which are devoid of any significance. Perhaps if we think of the proposal as assigning to them as a specific psychological role, which is part of the experience, it is less clear that there is any experiential contrast along the lines I am suggesting. For example, as noted above, according to Deonna & Teroni, Jamesian sensations ultimately constitute a unified feeling of bodily action readiness, a unified sense of one's body being poised for action (e.g. for flight or attack in fear), which amounts to a specific form of bodily awareness of value. Maybe, one might think, the intuition I am pushing is undercut if we think of them in this way.

However, this reply misses the point. As far as I can see, the objection remains unaffected by any proposal according to which Jamesian sensations are experienced as playing a particular psychological role. As accounts of emotional feeling these proposals still fail inasmuch as they ultimately understand it to be a type of proprioceptive sensation. Whether or not Jamesian sensations present themselves as poising our bodies for action and as thereby disclosing value properties, or as playing any other psychological role, they are at bottom sensations of muscular, autonomic and endocrine changes and as such lack the specific qualitative character that is pre-theoretically essential to emotional feeling. Such interpretations render them no more intelligible as being characteristically personal and as occupying a phenomenological location *different* from somatosensory experience than the original Jamesian proposal.[12] It thus does not make any difference in this context whether we ascribe to Jamesian sensations a particular role or significance. Somatosensory experience is simply the wrong type of phenomenally conscious occurrence to begin with. The Jamesian approach thus fails to elucidate the descriptive account of emotional feeling I have offered.

Now, in criticizing the Jamesian picture I have already elaborated somewhat further on the generic description of emotional feeling I initially

---

[12] Perhaps some will object that, understood as disclosures of value, they are intelligible as possessing a personal dimension. That is, if we understand the value properties in question as species of significance that are relative to a subject's cares and concerns, i.e. as value *for the person*. Cf. Sect. 2 in this chapter and Sect. 5 in Chapter 3. I agree that this may account for a personal dimension of emotional feeling. But it is not the kind of personal dimension at issue. As I suggested, the personal character of emotional feelings is inextricable from a specific phenomenological location which is distinct from that of Jamesian sensations. Whether or not they are understood as disclosive of personal value, *qua somatosensory* their phenomenological location is a different one.

provided by highlighting its specific qualitative character and personal dimension. In order to corroborate our grasp of this phenomenon and with a view to the discussion to follow, it will yet be useful to add some further content to this account and elaborate it in one additional respect. In the following subsection, I introduce a further popular way of construing the felt dimension of emotion, which is more sensitive to the relevant pre-theoretical considerations and provides some helpful further illumination of its qualitative character. In order to show that it gives an accurate picture of emotional feeling, I shall spend some time defending it against some common concerns.

1.2 Hedonic Tones

In the more recent debate on emotion, authors who recognize the Jamesian view as deficient often opt for a different approach according to which the felt dimension of occurrent emotion is fundamentally *hedonic*. As they propose, emotional feeling is essentially a specific form of (dis)comfort (e.g. Broad 1930, 229ff.; Greenspan 1988, chapter 1; 2004; Helm 2001, esp. chapters 2.2 and 3.4; 2002, 2009; Roberts 2003, 155ff.; 2013, 114f.; Slaby 2008, 121ff.; Schroeder 2007; Castelfranchi and Miceli 2009). At first sight, it may be tempting to suppose that this view runs into similar difficulties as the Jamesian picture. If, as one might perhaps think, the (dis)comfort in question is essentially the same as exemplified by ordinary sensory pleasures and displeasures, it seems to invite the same criticism. Thus, muscle aches and the gustatory pleasures of eating and drinking lack the distinctive personal dimension of *Gemütsbewegungen*, too. Considering the phenomenology of various paradigm emotions, it should be clear, however, that this is the wrong notion of (dis)comfort to invoke in this context. If we are careful not to operate with a too narrow conception of (dis)comfort, the view can be shown to possesses considerable plausibility.

Consider the way we ordinarily experience fear, sadness and guilt and compare it with experiences of joy, pride and satisfaction. To feel afraid, sad, or guilty is to be palpably affected in a way that seems unpleasant: we feel uneasy or uncomfortable. In feeling joyful, proud or satisfied, in contrast, the affectation is pleasant: we feel good. Here, we are not concerned with Jamesian sensations. The unease of fear is not an awareness of muscular tension, of accelerated respiration and heart rate, and of a rush of adrenaline. Nor is this discomfort mere sensory displeasure. Thus, the unease of fear seems very different from the discomfort of burns, blows or the unpleasantness of an empty stomach, for example.[13] In fear, we feel uncomfortable in a way that has a different qualitative character than ordinary sensory displeasures. It seems intimately related to a certain personal concern for our well-being or integrity and thus possesses a personal dimension that is missing in these latter cases. Relatedly, it seems to occupy a different phenomenological location than any of the former. As we might say, this discomfort is psychic rather than sensory.

These observations suggest that the view of emotional feeling as a form of (dis)comfort can help further refine the generic account of emotional feeling given so far. Ordinary experience provides support for the idea that the felt inner agitation of emotion is a form of (dis)pleasure that is characteristically personal and occupies a distinctive phenomenological location. While this picture is more sensitive to the relevant pre-theoretical intuitions than the Jamesian view, it can however seem problematic in a number of respects, too. In particular, like the Jamesian picture, it may seem unable to account for the variety of experiences that characterize our emotional lives. There are several familiar concerns which suggest that, as

---

[13] Jamesian sensations themselves often have a sensory hedonic dimension. For example, there is some displeasure to the sensation of a rush of adrenaline in fear. Yet, this sensory displeasure, too, seems crucially different from the (dis)pleasure characteristic of fear.

Some authors have thought to account for the (dis)comfort of occurrent emotion in terms of Jamesian sensations. Cf. Damasio (1994, 145). It seems to me that this is fundamentally mistaken. Cf. Roberts (2003, 155f.) and Schroeder (2007, 265f.) for criticisms of this approach. Arguably, the hedonic dimension of emotion is a matter of what I earlier referred to as the feeling of the 'lived body' (*leibliches Spüren*). Cf. Vendrell Ferran (2008, 168ff.). As I said, I will here set this topic aside.

There is also the view that bodily (dis)pleasure is to be modelled on emotional (dis)pleasure. Cf. Helm (2001, chapter 3.6; 2002) and Slaby (2008, chapter 6.3). On this view, bodily (dis)pleasure is like emotional (dis)pleasure in that it is intimately related to the subject's concerns. Helm motivates this view in part by means of the case presented in n. 11. I agree with him that the (dis)comfort of the first two experiences essentially refers to background concerns (for one's lover, for one's integrity) while these are at the same time bodily experiences. I would yet maintain that they differ from sensations such as ordinary toothaches and gustatory pleasures, which I here take to be the relevant contrast class. These lack the personal dimension of emotional (dis)pleasure. They are mere sensory (dis)pleasures, while the former are also partly psychic (dis)pleasures.

it stands, the view that emotional feeling is psychic (dis)comfort requires some further elaboration and defence.[14]

According to the explication I have offered of this view, it conceives of the felt dimension of a given emotion type (feeling afraid, angry, sad, joyful etc.) as a specific form of (dis)pleasure. There is an initial, perhaps rather obvious objection to this proposal. If it is understood as conceiving of each type of emotion as having a felt dimension that is *either* a pleasure *or* a displeasure, it obviously fails to take account of a very common type of emotional experience. Conceived in this way, it fails to accommodate for paradigmatic emotions that possess a mixed hedonic feel. Feeling nostalgic, melancholic and, perhaps, scornful involves a characteristic blend of pleasure and displeasure. However, it seems that this observation can easily be accommodated if the view is understood so as to explicitly allow for mixed hedonic tones. There is no reason why it should be understood as forbidding that the felt dimension of a given emotion type involves either pleasure, displeasure or a blend of the two. Once the view is qualified in this way, cases such as feeling nostalgic or melancholic no longer pose any difficulty.

While this qualification disperses one common worry with the idea that emotional feeling is (dis)comfort, several critics suppose that there are other reasons for thinking that it is falsified by the variety of occurrences that characterize ordinary experience. In particular, there is a concern which parallels the first consideration raised earlier against the Jamesian picture of emotional feeling. Thus, according to some authors, there are types of bona fide emotion whose occurrences simply do not involve any hedonic feel. As some have proposed, occurrences of anger and pity are not obviously pleasant nor unpleasant (cf. e.g. Tappolet 2000, 139; Deonna and Teroni 2012, 15). Sometimes admiration is mentioned, too

---

[14]To be fair, one may wonder whether any view that accords hedonic valence to emotion can accommodate for the large variety of phenomena that are treated as emotions in ordinary discourse and philosophical psychology. I take it to be important that the view I offer is able to accommodate for what are uncontroversial cases of paradigm emotions. Admittedly, in order to fully demonstrate this I would need to address further apparent concerns in addition to those discussed in this chapter. While I here lack the space to fully vindicate the idea that all paradigm emotions are forms of (dis)pleasure, below I respond to what I take to be the most significant concerns with the view.

(cf. e.g. Tappolet 2000, 139). The most commonly cited putative case of a hedonically neutral emotion is surprise.[15]

A further worry that is often voiced is that in the case of some emotions, hedonic tone may vary across occurrences. For example, while erotic love is often pleasant, it need not be. Indeed, unrequited erotic love is painful (cf. Vendrell Ferran 2008, 170). The converse point, one might perhaps think, is true of hatred.[16] However, as illustrated above, the view seems to assign a stable hedonic dimension to each type of emotion.

Let me address each of these further concerns in turn. While the first of them requires a somewhat more extensive treatment, I do not think that it ultimately poses a serious problem for a hedonic view of emotional feeling. As far as occurrences of anger, pity and admiration are concerned, there are strong reasons to maintain that they have a hedonic dimension. Thus, I do not share the intuition that these emotions involve no (dis)comfort. Consider the case of anger. Occurrent anger, it seems, essentially involves *bother*—it involves a certain sense of discomfort that is tied to one's upholding certain norms or standards. In anger, one feels uncomfortable inasmuch as something contravenes one's concern to be treated in a specific, respectful manner. This bother or discomfort has a personal dimension that crucially distinguishes it from ordinary bodily discomfort. I would maintain that something similar can be said of pity. Pity involves a certain personal distress or discomfort—one feels uncomfortable inasmuch as something contravenes one's concern for another's wellbeing. This hedonic dimension, again, is personal rather than somatosensory.

Now consider admiration. Occurrent admiration involves a rather profound positive feel. This feel is not a pleasure of any sensory sort; rather it is a case of felt positive resonance with one's values.[17] Admiration feels

---

[15] One might think of beatitude or bliss as another candidate. It is not supposed to have any valence on its traditional Christian understanding. However, I doubt that beatitude is intentional or has a target and thus counts as an emotion proper: we are not blissful at, of, about, for or over anything. For this reason, I here set it aside.

[16] One might in this context also think of some of Pfänder's remarks on attitudes (*Gesinnungen*). Cf. (1922, 11, 47). For example, an attitude of friendliness is usually accompanied by pleasure, but it can be unpleasant, too. Cf. also Vendrell Ferran (2008, 170). However, I take it that Pfänder's attitudes are not paradigm emotions.

[17] It might be more appropriate here to speak of one's valuings rather than one's values since the felt resonance is with a particular type of concern or attitude. I here keep with the term "value" since it seems to me more natural to use also in connection with this type of concern.

deep and there is something positive to that depth: a specific type of concordance or resonances with some of our values. (It is perhaps helpful to compare this comfort with the felt dimension of pride. In pride we feel good in a similarly deep way. However, there is also a clear experiential difference which has to do with the fact that in pride we ourselves are responsible for the satisfaction of those values.)

More generally, the claim that emotions such as anger, pity and admiration lack any hedonic phenomenology rests on a much too close assimilation of the discomfort characteristic of emotion to ordinary sensory pleasures and pains. In order to appreciate the plausibility of the idea that emotional feeling is psychic (dis)comfort, we must not model the latter on common cases of sensory (dis)pleasure, but rather acknowledge its characteristic personal dimension. That anger, pity and admiration do not involve any feeling that can readily be assimilated to ordinary physical pleasure or pain does not mean that their occurrences involve no hedonic feeling at all. To the contrary, if we avoid this rather narrow conception of hedonic tone, (dis)comfort can be recognized as a salient aspect of the way we commonly experience them.

Now, what I said about anger, pity and admiration does not seem to hold for surprise. It is certainly true that surprise is sometimes (though not always) mixed with occurrences of emotions that involve comfort or discomfort. For example, I may be pleasantly surprised to find that I have been invited to give a talk at a university to which I did not expect to be invited, in which case I am not just surprised but also delighted. Here, the feeling of surprise is intimately related to a feeling of comfort. In other cases, my surprise may be mixed with anger, e.g. when I receive an invitation from a university I am not keen to visit at all. In this case, it is closely tied to a sense of discomfort. But these observations do not show that surprise is ever *by itself* hedonic. If we focus on surprise itself, it seems that here we indeed have an example of a type of experience whose occurrences involve a felt agitation that is neither pleasant nor unpleasant.[18] To feel surprise—per se—is not to feel good or bad. Accordingly,

---

[18] (Dis)pleasure is often assumed to be an aspect of the occurrence of surprise itself. Cf. e.g. Deonna and Teroni (2012, 15). This picture fails to separate two distinct elements of the overall experience in these cases. If we compare them with occurrences of bare surprise and appreciate what is common

it seems that surprise constitutes a bona fide counter-example to the view that emotional feeling is psychic (dis)comfort.

Although the case of surprise cannot simply be dismissed in the same way as the previous alleged counter-examples, it is yet not obvious that it poses a genuine counter-example either. This is because one might think there are good reasons to doubt that surprise should be classed as a bona fide emotion to begin with. In fact, one might think that its very lack of hedonic tone is a strong reason to suppose that surprise is not an emotion.[19] The fact that occurrences of surprise are hedonically neutral suggests that they lack a feature that is central to our ordinary conception of emotion. In being neither pleasant nor unpleasant, occurrences of surprise crucially differ from those phenomena we recognize as paradigmatically emotional.

This response may sound ad hoc and revisionary. However, if one takes proper account of the phenomenal difference between surprise and those occurrences that classify as paradigmatically emotional and appreciates the place of hedonic tone within our pre-theoretical conception of emotion, the exclusion of surprise from the category of emotions seems warranted. In lacking hedonic tone, surprise lacks precisely the sense of being personally affected we find in paradigm emotions such as fear, anger, joy, sadness, guilt or admiration. The feeling of surprise is a felt contravention of a particular expectation. But it does not seem to relate us to genuine *cares* or *concerns* in the way that the former, hedonically qualified experiences do. Note, further, that someone, perhaps a subject of severe depression, who was in no way personally affected by significant events in her life and

---

to them, we have good reason to draw the distinction I propose. In this connection cf. Ekman and Friesen (2003, 35f.):

> Once you have evaluated the unexpected or misexpected event you move quickly from surprise into another emotion. "What a happy surprise," you say, not realizing that surprise itself is neutral in hedonic tone. It is rather the following emotion that gives a positive or negative tone to the experience, depending on the nature of the event. Surprise turns to pleasure or happiness if the event is or foretells something you like. Disgust greets the noxious or distasteful event. If the event is provocative of aggression, surprise yields to anger. And if the event poses a threat which you cannot obviously mitigate, you feel fear.

[19] Schroeder (2007, 259) recognizes hedonic tone as essential to emotion and therefore excludes surprises that are not mixed with occurrences of other emotions from bona fide emotional occurrences. As I noted above (n. 18), I do not think that comfort and discomfort are ever aspects of the occurrence of surprise. Thus, if hedonic tone is essential to emotion, we should exclude any occurrence of surprise from the class of emotional occurrences.

merely showed herself surprised by them would intuitively seem not to lead a psychological life worth the label "emotional" (cf. Schroeder 2007, 259). It seems to me that these considerations justify the exclusion of surprise from the domain of phenomena we are concerned with.

The apparent variability of hedonic tone across occurrences of a particular emotion type is similarly the result of a mistaken view of the phenomena. There is no doubt a sense in which unrequited love is unpleasant. However, acknowledging this does not require attributing a different hedonic dimension to the emotion in these cases but recognizing a distinct occurrence of disappointment or frustration. This distinct emotion is unpleasant in that it involves the frustration of particular erotic interests, including, perhaps, a more general interest to have a partner. These interests also inform the hedonic tone of erotic love: erotic love is pleasant inasmuch as its object is apprehended so as to positively resonate with these interests. Although the pleasantness of erotic love recedes into the background when it is unrequited, there is more to the overall experience than pain: it is usually a bittersweet affair. This suggests that there is a stable hedonic dimension to erotic love, which is positive.[20] As far as I can see, pleasant hatred can be given a similar treatment, though, in this case, we are dealing with a distinct occurrence of joy. While, like anger, hatred involves a characteristic sense of bother, we may often feel pleasure when the desire for revenge engendered by hatred is satisfied.[21]

To fully do justice to the impression of variability of hedonic tone that drives this objection, it is worth appreciating that the attribution to each type of emotion of a fixed hedonic dimension should not be thought to

---

[20] One might also think of erotic love as relatively stable attachment that is constituted by certain erotic interests. Cf. Roberts (2003, 291). On such a view, the positive resonance of something with these interests is distinct from the attachment so that erotic love cannot be conceived as having a hedonic dimension in the sense I propose. However, as Roberts suggests, insofar as genuine erotic love is an attachment, it is not an emotion. The pleasurable aspect of unrequired love is here to be conceived, like the painful one, as an aspect of a distinct emotional occurrence.

[21] As with love, hatred may also be a stable sentiment rather than emotion. Roberts (2003, 251) denies that hatred is based on a concern even when it is an emotion. I disagree. I find it hard to make sense of hatred of something which is not in one way or another apprehended as bearing on one's concerns. In typical cases, the target of hatred is apprehended in this way simply in virtue of what it is (rather than what it does). Some of what Roberts says seems to implicitly confirm this. As he says, when one hates a fly, one hates it simply because it is a fly, to which species one has an aversion. On a suitably liberal understanding of concerns (which Roberts himself adopts), an aversion towards flies is a (negative) concern.

imply that the felt agitation takes the exact same form in the case of each individual occurrence of a given emotion. Thus, we can still recognize a certain degree of variability with respect to the hedonic character of individual emotional occurrences. For example, the claim that occurrences of nostalgia and melancholy are united by a common admixture of pleasure and displeasure is compatible with allowing, for example, that in certain occurrences their characteristic discomfort may be more pronounced than in others. What is more, the ascription of a specific hedonic tone to a given emotion type may be thought to also allow for a certain degree of plasticity with respect to the way its individual occurrences unfold over time. Thus, it can accommodate for the observation that the (un)pleasant dimension of nostalgia or melancholy sometimes themselves varies in intensity and perhaps even in character, e.g. as one remembers further details of the past incidents at which the emotion is directed. If the view is sensitive to subtleties of this kind, it is not obvious to me that there is much substance to the charge of oversimplification at all.[22]

As these further remarks on the view that emotional feeling is hedonic tone will have shown, a lot of its plausibility is contingent on proper appreciation of the specific personal dimension I have attributed to emotional (dis)pleasure. The considerations I have here offered in connection with particular examples allude to the structure of this personal dimension by suggesting that it is in some sense tied to the fate of our cares and concerns. While I hope that these examples are reasonably intuitive, the picture offered so far is only a sketch and will be elaborated in more detail at a later stage of this work (cf. Sect. 2.1 in Chapter 4). Thus, if I have not managed to fully dislodge certain worries one might have with this view

---

[22] It is a difficult question to which extent hedonic tone can vary across occurrences of a single emotion type. Charland (2005) goes as far as to argue that the hedonic character of an emotional occurrence is fundamentally indeterminate and fixed entirely by second-order attention. I disagree with this rather radical claim. Although I wish to allow some room for attentional modulation, ordinary experience seems to me to provide strong support for the view that occurrences of a given emotion type are essentially pleasant or unpleasant in themselves. Each occurrence of fear essentially involves a characteristic unease which is not fixed by attention and can be attentionally modulated only in a limited sense.

While stressing that each emotion occurrence has an essential hedonic core, I should emphasize that the conception I am proposing is strongly opposed to any view of (un)pleasantness as an intrinsic, non-intentional feature of occurrent emotion, i.e. as a quale. Indeed, my main concern will be precisely to make sense of emotional (dis)comfort as being a mode of intentionality.

up to this point, the analysis I provide of hedonic tones at this later stage should help to further alleviate them.

Before I close these initial considerations on the felt agitation characteristic of emotion, I would still like to briefly comment on what may seem to be a further important dimension of emotional (dis)pleasure, which I have not yet addressed. As many authors suppose, the hedonic tone of emotions has motivational import. As some would maintain, to feel good or bad in having an emotion is *ipso facto* to be inclined towards a certain action or behaviour.[23] On this understanding, the displeasure of anger is inextricably intertwined with a certain inclination towards aggressive behaviour, for example; likewise, the displeasure of fear is extricable from an inclination towards avoidant behaviour (cf. e.g. Helm 2001, esp. chapter 3.4; 2002; Slaby 2008, esp. chapter 3.2).[24] According to a different conception, emotional (dis)pleasure is likewise recognized as motivationally significant, though here the assumed connection is less tight in that hedonic tone engenders a certain inclination to act.[25]

I believe that it is an interesting task to examine the nature of the link between the hedonic tone of emotion and motivation. This task might in fact be thought to be of direct interest to the idea that emotional feelings are significant qua intentional. It seems relevant to this idea since the first conception of this connection understands the (dis)pleasures in question as being identical to or comprising inclinations to act and those inclinations are plausibly themselves intentional phenomena. That said, I will here set this issue aside. This is because we have reason not to ascribe motivational import to the hedonic tones of emotions in general. And my primary interest in this investigation is to give an account of the psychological role of emotional feeling that illuminates what is common to the felt agitation characteristic of all emotions. Thus, while I am inclined to think that

---

[23] I distinguish inclinations to act from feelings of action readiness. Inclinations to act are prior to, that is, may lead to bodily preparation for action and thus to a sense of being poised for action.

[24] In this respect, it is similar to ordinary bodily pleasures and displeasures. Cf. e.g. Helm (2001, chapter 3.6), Slaby (2008, chapter 6.2), and Bain (2013) on bodily (dis)pleasure. Helm, Slaby and Bain understand hedonic tones to *rationally* motivate action. According to a different picture, hedonic tones merely trigger certain kinds of behaviour.

[25] I am not aware of any philosopher who explicitly espouses this view. But this is clearly a further position one might consider. Thus, it is widely held that sensory (dis)pleasure engenders inclinations to act. Cf. e.g. Graham (1993, 185).

the (dis)pleasure of at least certain types of emotion is intimately tied to motivation (e.g. the discomfort of anger and fear), there also seem to me to be several examples of emotional (dis)comfort which neither obviously constitute nor engender inclinations to act (e.g. the (dis)comfort of pride, regret, admiration and nostalgia).[26] Although it may still be interesting to explore the precise connection between emotional feeling and motivation in individual cases, this is of secondary importance as long as we are interested in giving an account of the significance of emotional feeling that applies to all emotions.[27]

2 Formal Objects

As I noted in the Introduction, an important insight of the renaissance of emotion within twentieth century philosophy of mind is that emotions take objects. Emotions are directed at things; they have 'particular objects' or 'targets': One is afraid *of* something, angry *at* someone or glad *that* some fact or state of affairs obtains. This observation is usually accompanied by a further one: emotions also have *formal objects*. In what follows, I explicate the idea of a formal object with a view to precisifying my understanding of the two intentionalist views of emotional feeling I will be concerned with in the main body of this work.

---

[26] This is in line with Roberts' view that not all emotions have what he calls "consequent concerns". Cf. (2003, 144), also Tappolet (2016, chapter 2).

[27] I have here not considered a further conception of emotional feeling, on which it is a kind of felt attraction or repulsion. Cf. Poellner (2016, 266f.), who takes Scheler to hold this view for the feelings involved in at least some emotions. I have also not discussed views on which the felt dimension of emotion can at least in part be characterized in terms of inclinations to act, where these are neither constituted by Jamesian sensations nor constituted or engendered by hedonic tones. Cf. e.g. Zamuner's (2015) conception of the polarity of emotion in terms of approach and avoidance. Though his conception is not explicitly concerned with emotional feeling, it arguably has some ramifications for the phenomenal aspect of at least some emotions (cf. ibid., 30). Both of these views likewise attribute to at least some emotional feelings a motivational dimension, though without explicitly construing them as a form of (dis)pleasure. While there is much to say about each of these proposals, I here lack the space to discuss them in detail. (I return to Poellner's view of emotional feeling in Sect. 3 in Chapter 3 and Sect. 1 in Chapter 4 and, very briefly, to Zamuner's view on emotional polarity in Sect. 1 in Chapter 4, n. 9.) I believe it is safe to set them aside, though, since these views do not seem to apply to emotional feelings in general either.

In very general terms, formal objects are *correlates* of specific types of intentional mental act or state.[28] Alternatively, one might say that they are the properties *proper to* specific types of mental act or state (cf. Goldie 2004a, 94; 2004b, 252). For example, the formal object of belief is truth or, as some would have it, the obtaining of a fact or state of affairs (e.g. von Hildebrand 1969 [1916], 38f.; 1953, 198; Mulligan 2010, 478). Other intellectual states are often assigned a different formal object. Thus, it is widely held that conjecture has the property of being probable, rather than the property of being true, as its formal object. Whilst individual occurrences of a given type of mental state may have different particular objects, its formal object is shared by all of them. There is a sense in which all beliefs are concerned with truth (obtaining) and all conjectures concerned with probability.

Emotions, too, are taken to have formal objects. These are constituted by certain 'thick' axiological properties. As is widely assumed, the formal object of fear is the property of being dangerous, the formal object of anger the property of being offensive. Sadness is commonly thought to have the property of being a loss as its formal object, while the formal object of joy is conceived as goodness (in some respect). In the case of pride, the formal object is often supposed to be the property of being ennobling or enhancing in terms of self-worth or dignity; in contrast, the formal object of shame is the property of being degrading or diminishing in this respect. As with truth and probability, the formal objects of emotions display a level of generality that allows them to be attributed to all instances of a given emotion type. Thus, it seems plausible to think that all instances of fear and joy are in a certain sense concerned with danger or goodness, respectively.

There are other candidates for the formal objects of emotions. More specifically, some authors suppose that the formal objects of emotions are response-dependent properties, that is, properties that are essentially linked to the very emotion whose formal object they are (cf. e.g. Goldie 2004a, 94; 2004b, 252). On this view, the formal object of fear is the property of being fearsome or frightening, the formal object of anger the

---

[28] I follow Teroni (2007, 396) in elucidating this idea. This account of formal objects draws on considerations on the nature of mental acts and states found in Husserl and Meinong.

property of being worthy of anger, the formal object of sadness (objective) sadness and that of pride pride-worthiness. I here deliberately opt for the traditional view, on which the formal objects of emotions are response-independent axiological properties. This view sits best with the common understanding of formal objects of other types of intentional states. Thus, usually belief is thought to have truth as its formal object, not credibility. Likewise, probability is commonly assigned as the formal object of conjecture, not the property of being worthy of conjecture. Moreover, and more importantly, the traditional view is more informative about what the range of particular objects of a given type of intentional state have in common. It is possible to specify a common theme behind the range of particular objects of a given intentional state type that better illuminates what unifies them than the corresponding view invoking a response-dependent property (cf. Prinz 2004, 61f.).

The specification of formal objects as correlates of or properties proper to specific types of mental state is not terribly informative and may not help much to illuminate the claim that emotions have formal objects. To add some more content to this claim, it is helpful to look more closely at the roles formal objects are commonly held to play in connection with occurrences of the corresponding intentional state. While there is no uniform agreement on this in every respect, I take it that most philosophers tend to agree on a basic characterization that recognizes three roles. In the following section, I briefly elaborate on these, focusing on the specific case of emotions. What I say there can however be generalized mutatis mutandis to other types of intentional state. Inasmuch as my main aim is to provide a basic explication of the roles of formal objects that is shared by most philosophers, I shall leave unsettled certain disputes regarding their correct explication. I take a more definite stance on some of these issues in the chapters to follow. I will close the discussion with some remarks on their ontological status and structure.

2.1 The Significance of Formal Objects

The formal object of a given type of emotion is commonly thought to play an essential role both with respect to the conditions of intelligibility of its instances as well as the conditions of their appropriateness or fittingness. Moreover, as most would add, it is specific to that type of emotion and thus serves to individuate it.

The role of the formal objects of an emotion with respect to the conditions of intelligibility of its instances is the most prominent role accorded to it (cf. Kenny (2003 [1963], chapter 9; de Sousa 1987, chapter 5; Teroni 2007, 403ff.). Consider the case of fear. It seems plausible to suppose that in order for someone's fear of a dog to be intelligible as such, she must apprehend the dog as being a certain way or as having certain properties. As the relevant intuition is commonly interpreted, she must apprehend it as posing a danger to her integrity or well-being or, as some would say, as having certain properties that bear a suitably intimate connection to danger, such as being aggressive or having sharp teeth. Unless she apprehends the dog in a way that is suitably related to the formal object of fear, it seems hard to make sense of her as being afraid of it. The formal object of fear thus provides a constraint on the intelligibility of individual instances of fear, that is, on their intelligibility as instances of fear that are directed at a specific object.

According to what used to be a prominent view in the earlier stages of their contemporary philosophical renaissance, emotions *presuppose* a cognition of their particular objects as instances of their formal object if they are to be intelligible as directed at them. On this view, in having an emotion we take its object to be valuable in a particular way, where this is a cognitive precondition of the emotion (cf. Kenny 2003 [1963], chapter 9; de Sousa 1987, chapter 5; Müller 2017, 286ff.). Various philosophers, notably proponents of AR, reject this reading, maintaining that for an emotion to be intelligible its object must merely be apprehended as being a certain way that is intimately related to, but distinct from, its formal object (cf. esp. Teroni 2007, 403ff.). On this alternative picture, emotions do not presuppose evaluative cognitions of their particular objects. For now, I shall leave open which of these two readings of the intelligibility constraint provided by formal objects is correct. I will settle this issue in Sect. 5 in Chapter 3.

The second role played by formal objects is easily illustrated by considering our ordinary critical practice regarding emotions. We assess emotions as *fitting* or *unfitting*. Moreover, it seems that in doing so we are guided by a standard provided by their formal object. There is a straightforward sense in which a person's fear of a dog seems fitting if the dog poses a danger to her and unfitting if it does not. Another way of putting the same point is in terms of the notion of *correctness*. Fears directed at things that are dangerous are correct, whilst those that are directed at things that are not dangerous are incorrect. In short, fear is fitting (correct) if and only if its particular object is dangerous.

Perhaps it will seem that, in contrast to the observation that the formal objects of emotions provide conditions of their intelligibility and fittingness, it is not as obvious that they also individuate them. Thus, it can seem that certain emotions share their formal objects with others. As Teroni (2007, 401f.) has noted, fear might be thought to share its formal object with excitement or, perhaps more plausibly, a particular type of thrill. There seems to be a specific form of thrill which is engendered specifically by what is dangerous.[29] However, upon closer inspection, these emotions constitute no actual counter-examples to the individuation claim. It seems fairly plausible to suppose that, in contrast to the formal object of fear, the formal object of excitement is a certain type of positive significance—a specific kind of good or benefit (in a sufficiently broad sense). In the case of certain forms of excitement which we refer to as thrills, this type of benefit may be exemplified by dangerous situations. In accordance with this understanding, we can allow that there is a particular form of excitement that has as its formal object a specific kind of benefit exemplified by danger. However, in contrast to fear, excitement is never concerned with danger *simpliciter*, but always with a specific form of positive significance. Teroni (ibid., 402f.) also argues that we cannot properly distinguish the formal objects of shame and contempt either. On his view, both emotions have as their formal object a distinctive kind of worthlessness we refer to with the term 'shameful'. I think this claim can be challenged, too. I would maintain that the formal object of shame is a form of degradation which

---

[29]Teroni in fact mentions a specific form of thrill that is engendered specifically by what is frightening. Here, the supposition is that, whilst one might distinguish the formal object of fear from that of excitement if one takes it to be the property of being frightening (rather than being dangerous), this move won't work in the case of the specific type of thrill in question. I think we can deny that any form of thrill is a counter-example to the individuation claim (without revising our attribution of danger as formal object to fear) if we suppose, as I think is very plausible, that thrill is always a form of excitement.

is constituted in part by an incongruence with certain norms or standards upholding which matters to one's self-worth. The formal object of contempt is a degradation that involves incongruence with certain norms or ideals one upholds, too. However, this degradation is not as intimately related to self-worth, since contempt is typically directed at others. It is only so related when contempt is directed toward oneself. Moreover, and more importantly, the formal object of contempt also involves incongruence with a concern that those who do not live up to those norms do not claim a status equal to those who do.[30] Incongruence with this concern is not part of the formal object of shame. One can be ashamed or oneself (or someone else closely associated with oneself) without apprehending oneself (the other) as claiming a status equal to those who abide by the norms one sees oneself (her) as violating. Relatedly, that shame of someone is fitting does not imply that contempt towards her is fitting, too. More generally, I think that putative counter-examples against the individuation claim can be successfully dealt with if one considers carefully enough which formal object the emotion in question is most plausibly assigned. Thus, I shall here further suppose that the formal object of an emotion also individuates it.

One important implication of the notion of the formal object of an emotion, as I have here explicated it, is that the exemplification of properties such as being dangerous, being offensive and being a loss must be to some extent independent of emotions enjoyed towards things exemplifying them. The role of formal objects in determining the fittingness conditions of the corresponding emotion presupposes that value properties are metaphysically sufficiently robust to provide a standard of correctness for its instances. This is incompatible with the claim that they depend for their exemplification on the very emotion whose fittingness is at issue. Accordingly, the account of formal objects offered here involves what may seem to be a substantial commitment. It presupposes that formal objects display a certain degree of objectivity and, in this sense, a certain form of axiological realism. In the remainder of this section, I add a few comments on this implication.

---

[30]The crucial role of this concern in contempt is discussed in an illuminating way by Roberts (2003, 255f.). I say more about the idea of (in)congruence in Sect. 2 in this chapter. Cf. also Sect. 5 in Chapter 3.

2.2 Axiological Realism

Inasmuch as a commitment to a realist understanding of the formal objects of emotion is implicit in ordinary critical practice, such an understanding seems warranted in the context of a project that is principally concerned to explicate the manifest image of emotion. This is not to deny, however, that there may be good reasons to suppose that this commitment stands in need of defence. There are various familiar philosophical concerns with value realism which can seem to exert considerable pressure on this view. Indeed, while most philosophers in the debate to which I intend to contribute wish to be largely faithful to the manifest image of emotion, they are at the same time sensitive to (at least some of) these concerns and attempt to answer them in one way or another. Thus, the view that emotional feeling is receptivity to value can be seen to be in part an attempt at defending a commitment to a realist understanding of formal objects against a common epistemological worry. According to this worry, the only way we could possibly have access to value properties would be via some special quasi-perceptual faculty which is tailor-made to provide access to value (cf. e.g. Mackie 1977, 38f.; Smith 1994, 25; Tappolet 2000, 67f.). The claim that emotional feelings constitute a specific type of value impression is in part intended to offer a non-mysterious epistemology of value and thus to contribute to vindicating value realism.[31]

I agree that a realist understanding of formal objects requires some defence. At the same time, it is important to be clear on the precise metaphysical commitments implied by the understanding of emotional fittingness supposed here. Thus, I think that certain traditional worries with an objectivist view of value may seem much less pressing in the present context once we appreciate that this understanding is committed only to a quite weak form of axiological realism. This itself may not be sufficient to answer concerns regarding our epistemic access to formal objects. At the same time, if we assume the weak realism I have in mind, these should not be thought to pose a serious threat either. That is, while the discussion to follow suggests that AR falls short of a plausible epistemology of value,

---

[31] At least part of the idea here is simply that emotions are a perfectly familiar aspect of our mental lives. However, proponents of AR usually do not leave it at that. Cf. Tappolet (2000, chapters 6 and 7) and Döring (2004, chapters 8 and 9).

I will ultimately show that it is possible to respond to these concerns by offering a different picture of our epistemic access to formal objects once their ontological structure is properly understood.

In order to convey the type of minimal realism about formal objects that I have in mind, let me briefly indicate what I take to be the most plausible way of understanding the type of property in question. Consider, for example, the property of being dangerous. This property is, quite plausibly, a relational property: for something to be dangerous is, roughly, for it to have a certain potential to harm something. Often, it is supposed that this potential for harm is a potential for harm to one's integrity or well-being. While this understanding arguably makes sense of the most common cases of fear, it however seems much more plausible to think of it as, more generally, the potential to harm *something one cares about* or *is attached to*. When I am afraid that the impending rain might seriously damage my copy of *The American*, which I inadvertently left on the garden table, my fear is not concerned with potential harm to my integrity or well-being (at least in the narrow sense in which these are usually construed), but rather to a particular material item that I am attached to. This suggests a rather natural account of danger: danger is a form of negative relevance to things *qua things that I care about*. For something to be dangerous is for it to be *bad* insofar as it incongruent with a certain concern of mine. More generally, the axiological character of formal objects consists in the positive or negative relevance—the congruence or incongruence—of their bearer with particular cares and concerns.[32]

To further illustrate this proposal, note that something very similar can be said about the formal object of sadness. Loss is, roughly, the relational property of failing to keep or continue to have something. The fact that, insofar as here the term "loss" specifies the formal object of sadness, it refers to an axiological property, plausibly has to do with the fact that the failure in question is a failure to keep or continue to have something that *one cares*

---

[32]This echoes appraisal theories of emotion in psychology. Cf. Reisenzein's (2009) explication of the appraisal-theoretic notion of relevance detection. It is very similar also to the view of formal objects endorsed by Helm (2001, chapters 2 and 3) and Düringer (2014, chapter 6). At least some of what Slaby (2008, chapter 5, esp. 5.3), Roberts (2003, esp. 147), and Döring (2004, chapter 8) say suggests that they are sympathetic to this approach, too. Nussbaum's (2001) view of the type of evaluation involved in emotion seems very close as well. Cf. (ibid., 30ff.). Slaby (2007, 2008, chapter 5, esp. 5.3) relates this approach to Heidegger's (1962 [1927]) account of fear.

about (cf. Prinz 2004, 61f.). In the axiological sense of the term, losses are essentially negatively relevant to one's concerns. A similar reading can be given of the property of being offensive, understood as the formal object of anger. Anger is concerned with what is offensive in the sense of what violates norms or standards that are *one's own*, i.e. norms or standards one *upholds* and thus *cares about*. Again, the badness implicit in the formal object of anger can be thought to reside essentially in its incongruence with particular concerns. What I said about the formal objects of shame and contempt in the foregoing subsection conforms to this view, too. The degradation in each case is a matter of incongruence with certain norms one endorses and is attached to. In contrast, the formal object of joy—goodness (in some respect)—can be identified with positive concern relevance: in this context, "good" refers to the congruence of some event or state of affairs with some of one's cares.

It is worth stressing that a view of formal objects as being relative to an individual's evaluative perspective in this way is entirely compatible with their recognition as sufficiently objective to provide standards of fittingness for a given emotion. Whether or not something positively or negatively bears on one's cares and concerns is independent of whether one enjoys a particular emotion directed at it. Moreover, it plausibly does provide a standard of fittingness for the corresponding emotion. Thus, if, in the above example concerning the formal object of fear, the impending rain bears the potential to harm what I care about, this makes it fitting for me to fear it. Similarly, if it lacks any such potential, it seems unfitting for me to fear it. To be fair, some philosophers find fault with this proposed understanding of the formal objects of emotion. For example, some proponents of AR reject the view as too subjectivist to provide sufficiently robust conditions of emotional appropriateness (cf. e.g. Slaby 2008, chapter 8, esp. 8.4).[33] It seems to me that this concern is misguided and that there is sufficient reason to accept the view of the formal objects of emotion I have outlined here. However, this will be easier to appreciate once I have settled the question, noted above, regarding the intelligibility conditions of emotions. What makes this view compelling, I think, is in large part that it can be seen to be congenial to a certain refined view of

---

[33] Some would disagree with this understanding on other grounds. Cf. von Hildebrand (1969 [1916], 37ff.; 1953, chapter 18) on value responses. Cf. also Sect. 5 in Chapter 3, n. 42.

the significance of formal objects, which will emerge in the context of assessing AR.

In discussing AR in the chapter to follow, I will not be committed to this view of formal objects. Thus, I will initially remain neutral with respect to different possible accounts that are compatible with the role of formal objects as I have here explicated it. Once I have refined my account of this role at the end of the following chapter, I will endorse this view for the remainder of the discussion.

Perhaps my proposed understanding of formal objects and the epistemology of value I shall propose in Chapter 5 will not be sufficient to dislodge certain rather deep-seated worries with any form of axiological realism.[34] However, they should be sufficient to disperse some of the central concerns in this area and thus render the proposed understanding of emotional fittingness amenable to many philosophers who are generally sympathetic to the manifest image of emotion.

3 Conclusion

The main purpose of this chapter has been to prepare the ground for the main dialectical thread. I precisified the initial generic description of emotional feeling in terms of the idea that emotional affectivity is a form of psychic (dis)comfort that possess a specific personal dimension. Moreover, I introduced the notion of a formal object of an emotion as an axiological correlate that provides conditions of intelligibility and fittingness for its instances and moreover serves to individuate it. These considerations provide important constraints on my subsequent discussion of the view that emotional feeling is receptivity to value as well as on my explication of the alternative intentionalist view I will be recommending in its stead. In assessing AR and developing PT I will be presupposing that emotional feeling is essentially hedonic in the sense explicated. Moreover, I will understand AR as conceiving of the felt aspect of emotion as a receptivity

---

[34] One might also think that this understanding is incomplete unless more is said about the cares and concerns to which it centrally appeals. I will not be able to take up the question of what it is to care for or value something in any detail within the confines of this investigation. In this connection, cf. e.g. Helm (2001, chapters 2 and 3) and Naar (2013, 2018).

to its formal object. Correspondingly, PT will be understood as conceiving of emotional feelings as responses to their formal object.

I should add that the considerations I have offered are not entirely preliminary in that they already rule out certain versions of AR from further consideration in the chapter to follow. As I have argued, versions of AR that conceive of emotional feelings as Jamesian sensations mischaracterize them to begin with. I will thus set these versions aside in what follows. In this context, I should also mention that my identification of the formal objects of emotions with response-independent axiological properties further narrows the scope of views under consideration by excluding versions of AR that conceive of emotional feelings as disclosing response-dependent properties (cf. e.g. Weberman 1996 (for at least some emotions); Zagzebski 2003; Döring 2004, chapters 8 and 9).[35] Indeed, in this respect, my understanding of AR might seem too narrow inasmuch as I here purport to address the general tendency to think of emotional feeling as receptivity to value. However, while this understanding of AR may be somewhat procrustean, it is still a representative version of this approach. Moreover, the most central difficulty I note with AR in the following chapter also arises for views that conceive of emotional feelings as presenting response-dependent properties.

References

Arnold, Magda. 1960a. *Emotion and personality*, vol. 1. New York: Columbia University Press.
Arnold, Magda. 1960b. *Emotion and personality*, vol. 2. New York: Columbia University Press.

---

[35]Tappolet (2000) can seem to fit this description as well, though, on her view, properties such as the fearsome or prideworthy are ultimately monadic axiological properties. Poellner (2016) may seem to be a further advocate for at least some emotions, though, as I read his reconstruction of Scheler's and Sartre's view on emotion, he takes the values emotionally disclosed not to be response-dependent either. Cf. his remarks on their conception of value (ibid., 264ff.). In this connection cf. also Dokic and Lemaire (2013) on the distinction between views that assimilate emotions to perceptual experiences of response-independent values and those that assimilate them to perceptual experience of response-dependent values.

Bain, David. 2013. What makes pains unpleasant? *Philosophical Studies* 166 (1): 69–89.
Broad, Charlie D. 1930. *Five types of ethical theory*. London: Routledge and Kegan Paul.
Cannon, Walter. 1927. The James-Lange theory of emotions: A critical examination and an alternative theory. *American Journal of Psychology* 39: 106–124.
Cannon, Walter. 1929. *Bodily changes in pain, hunger, fear and rage*, 2nd ed. New York: Appleton.
Castelfranchi, Cristiano, and Maria Miceli. 2009. The cognitive-motivational compound of emotion. *Emotion Review* 1 (3): 223–231.
Charland, Louis. 2005. Emotion experience and the indeterminacy of valence. In *Emotion and consciousness*, ed. Lisa Feldman Barrett, Paula M. Niedenthal, and Piotr Winkielman, 231–254. New York: Guilford Press.
Cobos, Pilar, María Sánchez, Carmen García, María Nieves Vera, and Jaime Vila. 2002. Revisiting the James versus Cannon debate on emotion: Startle and autonomic modulation in patients with spinal cord injuries. *Biological Psychology* 61: 251–269.
Cova, Florian, and Julien Deonna. 2014. Being moved. *Philosophical Studies* 169 (3): 447–466.
Damasio, Antonio R. 1994. *Descartes' error*. New York: Gossett/Putnam.
Damasio, Antonio R., Thomas J. Grabowski, Antoine Bechera, Hanna Damasio, Laura L.B. Ponto, Josef Parvizi, and Richard D. Hichwa. 2000. Subcortical and cortical brain activity during the feeling of self-generated emotions. *Nature Neuroscience* 3 (10): 1049–1056.
Deonna, Julien, and Fabrice Teroni. 2008. *Qu'est-ce qu'une émotion?*. Paris: Vrin.
Deonna, Julien, and Fabrice Teroni. 2012. *The emotions*. London: Routledge.
Deonna, Julien, and Fabrice Teroni. 2014. In what sense are emotions evaluations? In *Emotion and value*, ed. Sabine Roeser and Cain Todd, 15–31. Oxford: Oxford University Press.
Deonna, Julien, and Fabrice Teroni. 2015. Emotions as attitudes. *Dialectica* 69 (3): 293–311.
Descartes, René. 1931. The passions of the soul. In *The philosophical works of descartes*, vol. 1. Trans. E. S. Haldane and G. R. T. Ross. New York: Dover. Original edition: Descartes, René. 1649. *Les passions de l'âme*. Paris: Henri le Gras.
de Sousa, Ronald. 1987. *The rationality of emotion*. Cambridge: MIT Press.
Döring, Sabine. 2004. *Gründe und Gefühle*. Habilitationsschrift (Second book). Duisburg-Essen University.

Dokic, Jerôme, and Stéphane Lemaire. 2013. Are emotions perceptions of value? *Canadian Journal of Philosophy* 43 (2): 227–247.
Düringer, Eva. 2014. *Evaluating emotions.* Basingstoke: Palgrave Macmillan.
Ekman, Paul, and Wallace V. Friesen. 2003. *Unmasking the face.* Los Altos, CA: Malor Books.
Frijda, Nico. 1986. *The emotions.* Cambridge: Cambridge University Press.
Frijda, Nico. 2007. *The Laws of emotion.* Mahwah, NJ: Lawrence Erlbaum.
Goldie, Peter. 2004a. Emotion, feeling and knowledge of the world. In *Thinking about feeling*, ed. Robert Solomon, 91–106. Oxford: Oxford University Press.
Goldie, Peter. 2004b. Emotion, reason and virtue. In *Emotion, evolution and rationality*, ed. Dylan Evans and Pierre Cruse, 249–267. Oxford: Oxford University Press.
Graham, George. 1993. *Philosophy of mind.* Oxford: Blackwell.
Greenspan, Patricia. 1988. *Emotions and reasons.* New York, London: Routledge.
Greenspan, Patricia. 2004. Emotions, rationality and mind/body. In *Thinking about feeling*, ed. Robert Solomon, 125–134. Oxford: Oxford University Press.
Heidegger, Martin 1962. *Being and time.* Trans J. Macquarie and E. Robinson. New York: Harper & Row. Original edition: Heidegger, Martin 1927. *Sein und Zeit.* Tübingen: Max Niemeyer.
Helm, Bennett. 2001. *Emotional reason.* Cambridge: Cambridge University Press.
Helm, Bennett. 2002. Felt evaluations: A theory of pleasure and pain. *American Philosophical Quarterly* 39 (1): 13–30.
Helm, Bennett. 2009. Emotions as evaluative feelings. *Emotion Review* 1 (3): 248–255.
Hohmann, George W. 1966. Some effects of spinal cord lesion on experienced emotional feelings. *Psychophysiology* 3: 526–534.
James, William. 1884. What is an emotion? *Mind* 9: 188–205.
James, William. 1891. *The principles of psychology*, vol. 2. London: MacMillan.
Kenny, Anthony. 2003. *Action, emotion and will.* 2nd ed. London: Routledge and Kegan Paul. (Original edition 1963).
Mackie, John L. 1977. *Ethics.* London: Penguin.
Müller, Jean M. 2017. How (not) to think of emotions as evaluative attitudes. *Dialectica* 71 (2): 281–308.
Müller, Jean M. 2019. Dietrich von Hildebrand. In *Routledge handbook of phenomenology of emotions*, ed. Thomas Szanto and Hilge Landweer. London and New York: Routledge. (Forthcoming).
Mulligan, Kevin. 2007. Intentionality, knowledge and formal objects. *Disputatio* 23 (2): 205–228.

Mulligan, Kevin. 2008. Scheler: Die Anatomie des Herzens oder was man alles fühlen kann. In *Klassische Emotionstheorien von Platon biss Wittgenstein*, ed. Hilge Landweer and Ursula Renz, 589–612. Berlin: de Gruyter.

Mulligan, Kevin. 2009. On being struck by value. In *Leben mit Gefühlen*, ed. Barbara Merker, 141–161. Paderborn: Mentis.

Mulligan, Kevin. 2010. Emotions and values. In *Oxford handbook of the philosophy of emotion*, ed. Peter Goldie, 475–500. Oxford: Oxford University Press.

Naar, Hichem. 2013. A dispositional theory of love. *Pacific Philosophical Quarterly* 94 (3): 342–357.

Naar, Hichem. 2018. Sentiments. In *The ontology of emotions*, ed. Hichem Naar and Fabrice Teroni, 149–168. Cambridge: Cambridge University Press.

Nussbaum, Martha. 2001. *Upheavals of thought*. Cambridge: Cambridge University Press.

Pfänder, Alexander. 1922. *Zur Psychologie der Gesinnungen*. Halle: Niemeyer.

Poellner, Peter. 2016. Phenomenology and the perceptual model of emotion. *Proceedings of the Aristotelian Society* 116 (3): 261–288.

Prinz, Jesse. 2004. *Gut reactions*. Oxford: Oxford University Press.

Reisenzein, Rainer. 2009. Relevance detection. In *Oxford companion to the affective sciences*, ed. David Sander and Klaus Scherer, 339–340. Oxford: Oxford University Press.

Roberts, Robert C. 2003. *Emotions*. Cambridge: Cambridge University Press.

Roberts, Robert C. 2013. *Emotions in the moral life*. Cambridge: Cambridge University Press.

Rosenthal, David. 1983. Emotions and the self. In *Emotion*, ed. Gerald E. Myers and K. D. Irani, 164–191. New York: Haven.

Scheler, Max (1973). *Formalism in ethics and non-formal ethics of values*. Trans M. S. Frings and R. L. Funk. Evanston, IL: Northwestern University Press. Original edition: Scheler, Max. 1913–1916. *Der Formalismus in der Ethik und die materiale Wertethik*. Halle: Max Niemeyer.

Schroeder, Timothy. 2007. An unexpected pleasure. *Canadian Journal of Philosophy* 32 (Suppl.): 255–272.

Slaby, Jan. 2007. Emotionaler Weltbezug: ein Strukturschema im Anschluss an Heidegger. In *Gefühle: Struktur und Funktion*, ed. Hilge Landweer, 93–112. Berlin: Akademie.

Slaby, Jan. 2008. *Gefühl und Weltbezug*. Paderborn: Mentis.

Smith, Michael. 1994. *The moral problem*. Oxford: Blackwell.

Stocker, Michael, with Elizabeth Hegeman. 1996. *Valuing emotions*. Cambridge: Cambridge University Press.

Tappolet, Christine. 2000. *Émotions et valeurs*. Paris: Presses Universitaires France.

Teroni, Fabrice. 2007. Emotions and formal objects. *Dialectica* 61 (3): 395–415.
Vendrell Ferran, Íngrid. 2008. *Die Emotionen: Gefühle in der realistischen Phänomenologie*. Berlin: Akademie.
von Hildebrand, Dietrich. 1953. *Christian ethics*. New York: McKay.
von Hildebrand, Dietrich. 1969. *Die Idee der sittlichen Handlung*. Special edition. Darmstadt: Wissenschaftliche Buchgesellschaft. Original edition: von Hildebrand, Dietrich. 1916. Die Idee der sittlichen Handlung. *Jahrbuch für Philosophie und phänomenologische Forschung* 3: 126–251.
von Hildebrand, Dietrich. 2007. *The heart*. South Bend, IN: St. Augustine's Press. (Original edition 1965).
Weberman, David. 1996. Heidegger and the disclosive character of the emotions. *The Southern Journal of Philosophy* 34 (3): 379–410.
Whiting, Demian. 2012. Are emotions perceptual experiences of value? *Ratio* 25 (1): 93–107.
Zagzebski, Linda. 2003. Emotion and moral judgment. *Philosophy and Phenomenological Research* 66 (1): 104–124.
Zamuner, Edoardo. 2015. Emotions as psychological reactions. *Mind and Language* 30 (1): 22–43.

3

Emotional Feeling as Receptivity to Value

Abstract The axiological receptivity view (AR) is critically assessed in some detail. I start by laying out the phenomenological motivation for the view. As proponents of the view tend to suppose, ordinary experience supports AR in that emotional feelings are commonly experienced as a type of impression or presentation of value. I show that AR is wrong about ordinary experience. An adequate view of emotional phenomenology does not represent them as presentations or impressions, but as 'feelings towards'. As I argue, feeling towards fundamentally differs from presentation in respect of its intentional features. I further explicate the relevant difference by noting that feeling towards is a *response* to certain aspects of its object. Expanding on this criticism, I show that emotional feelings are necessarily responsive to a specific value (their formal object) and can therefore not apprehend it since they already presuppose awareness of it. The chapter concludes by rejecting AR.

Keywords Presentation · Perception · Feeling towards · Value response · Formal object

Intentionalism about emotional feeling is the view that emotional feeling plays a significant role in our mental lives inasmuch as it is a specific mode of intentionality. On the most common version of this view, our sense of being affected in emotion constitutes an intentional mode that renders it intelligible as *epistemically* significant. The proposal that emotional feeling is receptivity to value (AR) conceives of it as a form of impression that constitutes direct epistemic contact with value. On this account, emotional feeling is structurally on a par with ordinary perception. In having emotional feelings we apprehend value in much the way that we become acquainted with sensory features of our environment in sense-perceptual experiences. By means of the felt dimension of emotions we come to be aware of exemplifications of their formal object in that these are 'given' to or presented to us.

In this chapter, I critically engage with AR and argue that this view is in serious conflict with the manifest image of emotion. After some brief further exposition, I lay out more carefully what I take to be a major motivation for AR (Sect. 1). In the main part of this chapter I then raise a number of objections to the view (Sects. 2 and 3). As I go on to argue, the manifest image of emotion is in fact in conflict with AR in that it depicts emotional feeling as an intentional occurrence of a fundamentally different kind. I propose that, according to ordinary experience and discourse, emotional feeling is 'feeling towards', an intentional mode that sharply contrasts with the mode of presentation (Sect. 2). Explicating the fundamental difference between feeling towards and presentation, I argue that, in contrast to the latter, feeling towards is form of psychological involvement that constitutes a response to specific aspects of its object, including an apparent exemplification of the corresponding formal object (Sect. 3). I respond to a few possible concerns with this account of emotional feeling (Sect. 4) and finally spell out some consequences of this discussion for an adequate understanding of formal objects (Sect. 5).

I should note that, in criticizing AR in this chapter, I focus on a particular set of considerations, which I take to be most important to an appreciation of the way in which the view conflicts with our ordinary conception of emotion. The particular considerations I focus on point towards several fairly salient points of tension between AR and the manifest image of emotion. Moreover, they directly indicate a different, more adequate view of emotional feelings as intentional and, in this respect, lay the ground for a more accurate interpretation of the idea that emotional feelings matter qua intentional.

As will quickly become apparent, the central line of thought in this chapter draws on the early realist phenomenological tradition, in particular the writings of Dietrich von Hildebrand (1969a [1916], 1953). It also echoes an argument offered more recently by Mulligan (2007, 222; 2010a, 234; 2010b, 485), which is inspired by this tradition. A succinct version of the argument offered by Mulligan is that emotions are not presentations (or any other form of apprehension) since they constitute a specific form of position-taking and presentations (apprehensions) are not position-takings. In some places, Mulligan suggests that it in fact follows directly from the positive or negative character of emotions (which, as I read him, is understood in hedonic terms) that they are position-takings (cf. 2007, 222; 2010a, 234; cf. also Sect. 1 in Chapter 4).[1] I fully agree with Mulligan's considerations. However, in order to properly appreciate the intuition that lies behind this proposal, it is very helpful to look more closely at the notion of 'feeling towards', at the directedness and responsive character of emotional feelings and develop this line of thought in somewhat more detail. To gain a proper grip on the relevant contrast, it seems important to me to carefully contrast emotional feelings with presentation, as I do in what follows. In elaborating this contrast, I provide various considerations which coincide to a considerable degree with certain supplementary considerations offered by Mulligan himself,[2] though I also refer directly to and adopt several ideas from von Hildebrand's writings. I properly explicate the notion of emotional feeling as position-taking in the following chapter on the basis of the positive characterization I here propose in the course of criticizing AR.

---

[1] A congenial line of thought is indicated by Deonna and Teroni (2012, 68; 2014, 23) who stress that there is a difference between perception and emotion in that only that latter are valenced experiences.

[2] Some of the considerations I offer can also be found, albeit in a slightly different and/or less developed form, in Teroni (2007), Brady (2007, 2011, 2013, chapter 3.5), Deonna and Teroni (2012, chapter 6; 2014, 2015), Whiting (2012), and Dietz (2018).

1 The Manifest Image of Emotion According to the Axiological Receptivity View

Before I show how proponents of AR interpret ordinary emotional experience, I would like to add two brief remarks by way of further exposition.

AR is primarily concerned with occurrences of emotion that are appropriate or fitting. Strictly speaking, the version of intentionalism which I am here examining conceives of the felt aspects of emotional occurrences as presentations of value only when the emotion is appropriate or fitting. (When it is not fitting, emotional feelings are thought to constitute mere presentations *as of* value.) Thus, when I say that AR understands emotional feelings as epistemically significant, it is really the feelings involved in fitting emotions which are accorded epistemic significance.[3] In this context, the fittingness of an emotion is assessed in terms of the way in which the particular object of the emotion axiologically presents itself in emotional feeling, i.e. in terms of whether it presents itself in the way it really is.

When I introduced AR at the beginning of this work, I noted that this view is widely thought to be a plausible rendition of certain aspects of the manifest image of emotion. In particular, many of its proponents seem to share an intuition according to which ordinary experience shows the felt agitation of emotion to be a value impression. In order to bring this intuition out a little more clearly, it is helpful to look at two sample passages from writers endorsing AR. This should also help further clarify my initial characterization of the view.

Consider the following quote from Husserl (1989 [1952], 196), who is—along with Meinong (1972 [1917])—one of the main pioneers of this view.

---

[3] Plausibly, fittingness itself does not suffice for the respective feeling to constitute epistemic contact with value. The mere fittingness of an emotion does not guarantee that it makes epistemic contact with value as opposed to being a 'veridical axiological illusion', which lacks a sufficiently robust connection to value to count as a case of epistemic contact. In this connection, cf. also Mulligan (2007, 221ff.; 2010b, 485).

In these acts [acts of pleasure and displeasure, JMM], the object is brought to consciousness as valuable, pleasant, beautiful, etc., and indeed this happens in various ways, e.g. in original givenness. In that case, there is built, upon the substratum of mere intuitive presenting, an evaluating which, if we suppose it, plays, in the immediacy of its lively motivation, the role of a value-"perception" [...] in which the value character itself is given in original intuition. When I hear the tone of a violin, the pleasantness and beauty are given originarily if the tone moves my feelings originally and in a lively manner, and the beauty as such is given originally precisely with the medium of this pleasure, and similarly is the mediate value of the violin as producing such a tone, insofar as we see it itself being played and grasp intuitively the causal relation which is founding here.

According to Husserl's description of aesthetic pleasure and displeasure,[4] these are comparable to sense-perceptual experiences in how they relate to value properties. In being moved or affected by the sound of the violin (as it moves one's feelings), its beauty or pleasantness is 'given'. Husserl here seems to be appealing to the idea that, as far as aesthetic pleasure and displeasure are concerned, emotional feeling presents value in much the way that sense-perceptual impressions present properties of the sensory environment. As I read Husserl, it is specifically the affective aspect of these emotions that is supposed to constitute a (quasi-)perceptual grasp of value. "[T]he tone moves my feelings" is a translation of "der Ton [bewegt] mein Gemüt" (1952, 186). Husserl here explicitly refers to the character of aesthetic pleasure as a way in which our sentimental mind is stirred.

A similarly suggestive, more recent phenomenologically motivated statement of AR is provided by Helm. In the following passage, Helm describes emotional feelings quite generally, referring explicitly to their hedonic character. As he proposes,

> [t]o feel good (be pleased) or feel bad (be pained) is to have the import of one's situation, as good or bad, impress itself on one. (2001, 80)

---

[4] Husserl here refers to the emotions of aesthetic pleasure and displeasure, which one might want to distinguish from their felt dimension (i.e. their characteristic (un)pleasantness or character as stirrings of the sensitive mind). Husserl does not seem to me to draw this distinction. At any rate, as I read him, what he has in view here is emotional feeling. Cf. my remarks in the main text below.

In claiming that import (that is, value) "impress[es] itself on one" Helm means to be alluding specifically to the way colours present themselves in perceptual experience:

> [W]e might say, the import of the situation – the dangerousness of the ball, its having this import given the import of the vase – impresses itself on us in our feeling a particular emotion, in something like the way colors impress themselves on us in perception. (2002, 16)

In this respect, he seems to appeal to the same phenomenological picture as expressed in the passage by Husserl: the felt aspect—in this case, the unpleasantness or sense of being pained—of one's fear of the baseball is a way of registering or apprehending disvalue; it is an impression of disvalue, an experience of its dangerousness being 'given'.[5]

These passages convey the phenomenological intuition that seems to make AR compelling to many authors and give some intuitive content to the notion of a *presentation* of value. In line with McDowell's (1996) characterization of perceptual experience, some authors also speak in this context of "openness" to value (cf. Dokic and Lemaire 2013). I here use the term "presentation" since it seems to me to be more directly evocative of the idea that value is 'given' in a manner paradigmatic of the way perceptible properties are apprehended in sense-perceptual experience (cf. also Chudnoff 2012). This use ultimately goes back to Meinong (1972 [1917]), who explicitly uses the term to characterize emotional experience.[6] When I occasionally speak instead of value impressions or appearances, it is this same idea that I have in mind.[7]

It is perhaps worth noting that not all of the philosophers I listed as proponents of AR in the Introduction explicitly appeal to phenomenological considerations of this type. Moreover, there are additional, in particu-

---

[5] This is not all there is to Helm's view, since he also thinks of emotional feelings as forms of assent. Cf. Sect. 2 in Chapter 1, n. 11 and Sect. 1 in Chapter 4, n. 17.
[6] For helpful expositions of Meinong's account of emotion, cf. Findlay (1935) and Vendrell Ferran (2009).
[7] This use of the terms also seems to me to be in line with some of Husserl's claims. Husserl occasionally also speaks of emotion as involving value appearances: "In a certain sense […] something appears in the valuing acts (emotions, JMM) as well, in them appear […] not merely the objects which have value, but the values as such" (1988, 323, own transl.).

lar epistemological, motivations for holding this view (cf. Sect. 2.2 in Chapter 2). However, it is certainly notable that many contemporary proponents of AR, including authors who do not explicitly offer phenomenological considerations of this sort, in one way or another link themselves with Husserl, Meinong and other writers in the phenomenological tradition in whose work this intuition has been argued to occupy a prominent place.[8] I here take this intuition to be the most salient motivation for holding (AR).

On the face of it, the idea expressed in the passages by Husserl and Helm may appear rather compelling. Perhaps this is because it seems that, as far as ordinary emotional experience is concerned, there is clearly an intimate connection between our sense of being affected and awareness of value. It is hard to imagine the one without the other. Although this suggests that AR possesses a certain phenomenological plausibility, it is important to consider the way in which the felt inner agitation of emotion presents itself in ordinary experience sufficiently closely, however. Closer examination clearly shows that the phenomenological picture I have illustrated is much less compelling than it initially seems. As I hope will become apparent in the remainder of this chapter, there are good reasons to think that AR is at odds with the phenomenology of emotion.

---

[8] For example, Tappolet (2000, chapter 6) explicitly refers to Husserl and Meinong. She also refers to Scheler (1973 [1913–1916]), supposing his view of 'value feelings' refers to emotional feeling. This reading also in part inspires Poellner's (2016) account, who moreover refers to Sartre (esp. 1999 [1983], 2002a [1939], 2002b [1939], 2003 [1943], 2004 [1936–1937]) in developing his qualified version of AR. Interestingly, although Scheler uses the term "emotional" in connection with value feelings, as I read him, he draws a sharp distinction between them and occurrent emotion. Cf. Scheler (1973 [1913–1916], esp. 255ff.). For this reading cf. also Mulligan (2008, 591ff.), Vendrell Ferran (2008, 205ff.) as well as Sect. 1 in Chapter 5. Poellner (2016, 267, n. 9) explicitly opposes this interpretation, though I won't be able to defend what I take to be the correct one here. There is also some controversy about how Sartre's views on emotion are to be interpreted. Cf. also Weberman (1996b). Weberman (1996a) and Slaby (2008, chapters 5 and 9) in large part base their versions of AR on a particular reading of Heidegger's account of emotion, esp. § 30 of *Being & Time* (1962 [1927]), which they take to support a phenomenological understanding of emotional affectivity much like the one illustrated above. Although Helm (2001, chapters 2 and 3; 2002, 2009) does not explicitly refer to Heidegger, his work displays a certain affinity to specific themes from *Being & Time*, which suggests that he might be influenced in part by a similar reading of his views on emotion. Though clearly an important and worthwhile task, I here lack the space to enter a more through discussion of the question of which classical phenomenological writers ultimately hold versions of AR. Relatedly, I also do not mean to suggest that, with the exception of von Hildebrand and Scheler, all the classical phenomenologists were committed to AR.

What I argue in the following section undermines the common, phenomenological motivation for AR and simultaneously provides a strong objection against the view. My discussion crucially draws on phenomenological observations and suggests that AR is in conflict with precisely that aspect of our ordinary conception of emotion which it primarily purports to capture. However, the considerations I present will not be concerned exclusively with the phenomenology of emotion. Rather, I will offer a broader criticism that draws on further, related aspects of our pre-theoretical conception of emotion. As we shall see, as we pre-theoretically conceive of emotional affectivity, to feel afraid, sad or joyful is to be psychologically involved with the world in a way one might think of as the exact opposite of presentation.[9]

2 How the Axiological Receptivity View Fails the Manifest Image of Emotion: Feeling Towards

Imagine perceiving a landscape.[10] There are various objects in front of you: houses, trees, a mountain in the background. Giving a naïve description of your visual experience, we might say that these objects are *presented* to you. The same goes for their properties: the redness of the roofs, the dark green of the trees, the shape of the mountain are all in a fairly straightforward sense presented to you. (Using Helm's expression, one might say that they 'impress themselves' on you.) Now, imagine that, as you perceive the

---

[9]The objection I raise against AR in the following section parallels a criticism offered by Whiting (2012, 97ff.). As Whiting argues, the phenomenology of emotional feeling recognizes no axiological impressions. While I agree with Whiting, it seems to me that his criticism is comparatively less compelling in that he fails to recognize that emotional feeling is ordinarily experienced as having intentional features that sharply contrast with impression or presentation. This makes a difference insofar as we aim to properly dislodge the phenomenological intuition driving proponents of AR.

There is also a similarity between my objection and the way in which Deonna and Teroni (2015, 306) contrast the phenomenology of emotion and the phenomenology of perception. Although, unlike Whiting, they offer an alternative account which resonates to a certain degree with my own considerations, I do not think the contrast is sufficiently worked out, however. Cf. also Sect. 3 in Chapter 4.

[10]The following example is inspired by von Hildebrand (1969a [1916], 10f.). Cf. also Reinach (1989, 295).

landscape, you also feel an emotion. Contemplating the scene in detail, intense joy wells up in you. In saying that joy wells up *in* you, we imply that it contrasts in respect of its phenomenological location with the perceived external scene. More specifically, the way you feel in having the emotion seems to be something 'inner'. At the same time, this feeling has a specific connection with the 'outer' scene: it is *directed toward* that scene. You feel good *about* the scene.

If this account is descriptively accurate, there is a salient phenomenological difference between emotional feeling and perception.[11] As a first pass, one might say that there is a different *direction* to the intentionality of each type of experience. Thus, von Hildebrand proposes that in perception, "the intention goes, so to speak, from the object to the subject: the object reveals itself to our mind, it speaks and we listen" (1953, 178).[12] Somewhat less figuratively, we might say that in perception your role is that of a recipient who registers what is presented. By contrast, it seems that the intentionality of your emotional feeling towards the scene has the opposite direction. Here, the 'intention' goes from the subject to the object: the pleasant feeling inside you is directed towards the external scene; it is you who 'speaks' (cf. ibid., 178).[13] Another way of putting this contrasting point is in terms of your feeling having a *target*. This notion represents your feeling as being *aimed at* something. Von Hildebrand's speech act-metaphor is somewhat more evocative, though, in that it invites a slightly richer characterization of this directedness. It invites thinking of emotional feeling as a position adopted towards an object: in having a positive feeling toward the landscape you are not simply registering the scene, but *take a favourable stand* towards it.

Since the contrast I am highlighting may be unfamiliar, it calls for further elucidation. Although the idea that emotional feeling is directed towards something or, in Goldie's (2000, chapters 2 and 3; 2002, 2009)

---

[11] In connection with the contrast that I am here elaborating, cf. also Salice's (2016, section 2.1.2) exposition of von Hildebrand's views on intentionality as well as Müller (2019, section 1.1).

[12] von Hildebrand is here actually concerned with a broader class of phenomena he calls 'cognitive acts', of which perception is a paradigm case. I think it is fair to read his description as being primarily aimed at the presentational character of perception, though.

[13] von Hildebrand's claim concerns all so-called "responses". I say more about the responsive character of emotion below.

terms, is 'feeling towards', has found its way into the current debate on emotion, so far relatively little attention has been paid to the specific sense of directedness at issue and how it differs from presentation. Indeed, it is sometimes supposed that in recognizing emotional feelings as feelings towards, we conceive of them in just the way proposed by AR. For example, in discussing Goldie's account of emotion, Deonna and Teroni suppose that feeling towards is essentially "the way in which the world is evaluatively presented to us through emotions" and that the term is ultimately "a mere placeholder for *whatever adequately fulfills the function of making the subject aware of evaluative properties*" (both quotes from 2012, 70, emphasis JMM; cf. also 2008, 73 and Tappolet's (2002) review of Goldie 2000). In fact, Goldie's own account of feeling towards sometimes shows strong affinities with AR.[14]

One might also doubt that what I have said so far by way of contrasting emotional feeling and presentation generalizes to all emotions. For example, in the case of an immediate reaction of fear to a sudden danger this contrast is not as easily set up. Here, it is less plausible to say that the emotion 'wells up in you' and contrasts in respect of its felt location with the external situation. Can we still characterize the felt aspect of immediate emotional reactions as being aimed at something? To show that we can and further elucidate what I have in mind, I will take a closer look at the locutions we deploy to ascribe objects to emotions and perceptions. This should help further clarify the relevant notion of directedness and the contrast between emotional feeling and presentation. Once it is clear how AR conflicts with an adequate understanding of the intentionality of

---

[14]Consider the following passage:

> [...] there is what I will call *feeling towards*, the feeling one has towards the object of one's emotion. For example, in fear I feel the dangerousness of the lion. (2002, 235)

> The second sentence specifies a type of feeling that makes the view look rather close to AR. Feelings of value are a form of receptivity to value. Cf. Scheler (1973 [1913–1916], esp. 257ff.), von Hildebrand (1969a [1916], 77ff.; 1969b [1922], 133ff.) and Mulligan (2004, 216ff.; 2007, 223ff.; 2009, 2010a, 232ff.; 2010b, 486f.). Cf. also Sect. 1 in Chapter 5. While I believe that Goldie also shares the intuition that drives my use of the term, he does not have a sufficiently clear grasp of the difference I am looking to highlight.

emotional feeling, I will then, in the positive part of this book, go on to elaborate on the claim that emotional feeling is position-taking.

While "directed toward" is often used technically to characterize all intentional phenomena, there is a more restrictive, ordinary use that captures what is specific to emotional as opposed to perceptual intentionality. On this use, the term is a near synonym of "aimed at" and applies only to some intentional phenomena.[15] More specifically, we can speak of joy, fear, indignation, jealousy, contempt, admiration and their felt aspects as directed toward (aimed at) something. In contrast, perceptions do not admit of this characterization. Thus, on this use of "directed toward", the following sentence seems anomalous:

Maria's anger/discomfort was directed toward Sam; and so were the visual perceptions she enjoyed as Sam approached

Compare, moreover, the prepositions we use in attributing objects to emotions and perceptions, respectively (cf. also von Hildebrand 1969a [1916], 10, n. 1). In the former case, we use prepositions such as "about", "at" and "over":

Sam is/feels glad about the scene in front of his eyes
Maria is/feels angry at Sam
George is/feels enthusiastic over his victory

These prepositions convey a direction towards an object. In this respect, they differ from the preposition "of", as used to attribute objects to perception:

Maria has a vivid perception of the landscape
Sam enjoys a visual experience of the mountains

---

[15] I do not offer "addressed at" as a possible synonym to avoid confusing the directedness of emotional feeling with a specific communicative role that is sometimes accorded to emotions. It is often supposed that emotions are adaptive in that they are communicated to others via their characteristic (e.g. facial) expressions. However, to specify the target of an emotion or emotional feeling is not to specify whom it is communicated to. Maria's anger/the way she feels may be directed towards Sam in a situation where it cannot be communicated to Sam (e.g. because Sam is absent).

Rather than conveying a direction towards an object, "of" here specifies what is registered. To be precise, "of" can also be used to attribute emotional objects:

Maria is/feels afraid of the approaching motorbike
John is/feels contemptuous of Peter

However, here the preposition conveys something different. Note that we can paraphrase these ascriptions by saying that the respective emotion or feeling is directed towards (aimed at) something. When "of" attributes objects of perception, no such paraphrase is possible. The same goes for ascriptions of objects to the two phenomena by means of "that"-clauses. Consider:

Peter is/feels glad that he got sight of the scene
George is/feels sad that the show has closed

These sentences contrast in the same way with sentences such as

Maria perceives that there is a mountain.

While the former can be paraphrased in terms of the emotion or feeling being directed at a certain state of affairs, the latter admits of no corresponding paraphrase.

These linguistic considerations illustrate the contrast I have in mind. Moreover, they suggest that it is not restricted only to specific emotional responses: we speak of emotions and their felt aspects as being directed towards (aimed at) something regardless of whether they arise slowly or as an immediate reaction.[16] To offer some additional elucidation of the

---

[16]Thus, it makes perfect sense to say of Maria's sudden reaction of fear in the face of an approaching motorbike that her fear/the way she feels is directed towards (aimed at) the approaching motorbike. Relatedly, I would maintain that there is also an *inner* feeling in such cases. Although at the time, our attention is fully directed outwards, we can later turn our attention inwards and appreciate our inner agitation at that time. Considerations along these lines hint at a further difference between emotion and perception in respect of *transparency*. On this issue, cf. also von Hildebrand (1969a [1916], 9ff.), Deonna and Teroni (2012, 69), and Poellner (2016, 271ff.). There is more to be said about this apparent difference and how it relates to the contrast concerning their intentionality. I

notion of directedness in play, I would like to supplement these considerations with some remarks on the relation between emotional feelings and reasons. This will show more clearly how the view I am elaborating is opposed to AR.[17]

3 Feeling Towards and Responsiveness

To make sense of the directedness of emotional feelings, it is useful to examine the role of emotional targets as reasons for them. More specifically, when having an emotion towards something, its target constitutes a reason for which we feel accordingly. We feel a certain way *in light of* some aspect of the emotion's target. This seems to be entailed by the feeling being directed toward this target. A different way of putting this claim is by saying that an emotional feeling is directed toward something *as a response* to it.[18]

I will shortly offer some support for this claim. Before I do this, let me add a few remarks on reasons for emotions and emotional feelings and indicate how I use the term "response" in this context. It is common in the philosophy of action and epistemology to distinguish between the reasons for which an agent acts (thinks, feels etc.) a certain way—motivating reasons—and reasons for her to act (think, feel etc.) this way—normative or justificatory reasons. Consider the following case: Maria is angry at Sam because he performed better than her in the final exam. That Sam performed better than her is a reason for which Maria is angry at him. It is something *in light of which* or, alternatively, *on occasion of which* she is

---

here set it aside, though, in order to focus on the more important task of explicating the notion of directedness.

[17] It is worth noting as a corollary that the above considerations on ordinary experience and ascriptive practice suggest that emotions are directed insofar as they involve directed emotional feelings. This seems especially plausible in light of the fact that we canonically use the same intentional locutions in our ascriptions of emotions and of their felt dimension.

[18] My use of the term "response" goes back to Scheler (1973 [1913–1916]) and von Hildebrand (1969a [1916], 1953). Cf. also Müller (2019, section 1.1) on Hildebrand's use of the term. In a similar vein, Dietz (2018) claims that thinking of emotions as having motivating reasons is to conceive of them as responses. For thorough explication of this use in connection with reasons for action, cf. Bittner (2001). Hornsby (2008) and McDowell (2013) also use the term to characterize actions performed in the light of a fact.

angry at him. In specifying the result of the exam as a reason for which Maria is angry we explain her emotion. This is not to say that her anger is thereby shown to be justified. The fact that Maria is angry for this reason does not entail that there is also a good reason to be angry at Sam. After all, his better performance in the final exam does not really speak in favour of being angry at him. Thus, motivating reasons for emotions are to be distinguished from normative (good) reasons for them. Note that the same distinction applies also in connection with the felt aspect of emotions. When Maria is angry at Sam because he performed better in the final exam, this is also the reason for which she feels angry towards him. While this reason explains how she feels, it is not a reason to feel that way.

In order to guard against a possible misunderstanding of the connection between the felt aspect of an emotion and its target, it is crucial moreover to distinguish motivating reasons from mere explanatory reasons or causes (cf. also Alvarez 2010, 35ff.; Bittner 2001, 77f.). We also often give causal explanations of emotions and emotional feelings that do not cite motivating reasons. Consider the following two examples of explanations of emotions:

Maria is/feels angry at Sam because she drank too much
Maria is/feels angry at Sam because he performed better than her

The former is a causal explanation of Maria's anger. This explanation cites a reason why Maria is/feels angry, but it does not specify *her* reasons for being/feeling angry at Sam, i.e. those (purported) aspects of the situation *in light of which* she is/feels angry. These are cited only in the second explanation: it is only in this case that "because" can be substituted by "in light of" or "on occasion of". As I use the term "response" in this context, it serves to attribute motivating reasons, not mere explanatory reasons. Although "response" can also be used to attribute mere explanatory reasons, my use of it is closer to the most common, everyday use of the term. That is, as I use it, saying that Maria's emotion or feeling is a response to Sam's better performance is tantamount to saying that she is or feels angry at him in light of his better performance.

As some philosophers have recently stressed, there is an important difference between emotion and perception in that only the former admit of justifying reasons (e.g. Brady 2007, 2011, 2013, 112f.; Deonna and Teroni 2012, 69 and chapter 8). Note that we can always request justifications for an emotion by asking "Why are you angry at/afraid of/enthusiastic over x?". Again, the same is true of emotional feelings ("Why do you feel angry at/afraid about/enthusiastic over x?"). Such questions, in contrast, seem not to make sense in the case of perceptions. "What is your reason for perceiving x?", construed as a request for a justification, is meaningless.[19] What is less often made explicit is that the same difference holds in respect of motivating reasons (cf. Müller 2017; Dietz 2018, as well as Mulligan 2010b, 485). If it is true that there is a difference in respect of justificatory "why"-questions, this already indicates that only emotions and emotional feelings admit of motivating reasons that are also normative reasons, since, after all, such requests enquire whether the subject's motivating reasons

---

[19] According to Poellner (2016), the fact that we can request justifications for emotions has to do with the nature of the axiological properties that emotions register. We request a justification when we are unsure whether the non-axiological properties on which they depend for their exemplification are themselves instantiated and thus whether the experience is veridical. Poellner claims that there is in fact no significant disanalogy with perception as long as we are concerned with perception of higher-order properties: we can likewise request a justification for why someone hears a chord as dissonant.

There are several things to say in response. Most importantly, though, Poellner's reply does not engage with the original worry. His apparent counter-examples to the disanalogy concern cases of aspect perception, ascribed by "perceive x as F", rather than cases of direct perception, ascribed by "perceive x". But the comparison, as stated above, concerns reason-requests for direct perception. To be fair, AR is sometimes understood also in terms of aspect perceptions rather than direct perceptions. I deal with this reading in section 4.

In discussing the disanalogy concerning justificatory reasons, Tappolet (2012, 231f.; 2016, 39f.) likewise appeals to the nature of the axiological properties allegedly registered emotionally. While accepting the dissimilarity, she thinks it is an artefact of their dependence on non-axiological properties, rather than revealing anything interesting about the nature of emotion that might conflict with a substantive similarity with perception. I doubt the cogency of this response, though I won't discuss it in more detail. As I hope the following will show, there is no prospect at maintaining that the admissibility of reasons is inessential to the nature of emotions or their felt aspects once we appreciate the essential connection between their intentionality and motivating reasons. On the plausible assumption that intentionality is an aspect of the nature of emotions/emotional feelings and perceptions, the fact that only the former admit of motivating reasons points towards an essential difference between them.

I here set aside a number of further issues concerning differences between the two in respect of their justificatory and rational import since they seem less important in order to get clear on the intentionality of emotional feeling. For more on this topic, cf. e.g. Brady (2011, 2013, chapter 3), Tappolet (2012, 2016, chapter 1), Pelser (2014), and Poellner (2016).

are also good reasons. Note, though, that when such "why"-questions are construed as a mere request for the subject's motivating reasons (regardless of whether they are also good reasons), there is a similar contrast in that they make sense only when asked about emotions or their felt aspects, not when asked about perceptions. Although we can request mere explanatory reasons or causes for perceptions by asking "why do you perceive *x*?", this question is non-sensical as an enquiry about the reasons for which someone perceives something.[20] What is more, the fact that emotions admit of motivating reasons has a direct bearing on the intentionality of emotion. As I noted at the outset of this section, it seems to be an aspect of the very directedness of emotions and their felt aspects that they are responses.

To see that the directedness of an emotion or emotional feeling implies that it is a response, we need to look once more at ordinary emotion ascriptions. Consider the following sentences:

*Peter is/feels glad about the scene, though he is not/does not feel glad because of the scene
*Maria is/feels afraid of the approaching motorbike, though she is not/does not feel afraid because of the motorbike
*George is/feels sad that the show has closed, though he is not/does not feel sad because of this fact

In all of these cases "because of" does not specify a mere explanatory reason, but a motivating reason. We can likewise formulate these sentences using "in light of" or "on occasion of":

*Peter is/feels glad about the scene, though he is not/does not feel glad in light of the scene
*Maria is/feels afraid of the approaching motorbike, though she is not/does not feel afraid on occasion of the motorbike
*George is/feels sad that the show has closed, though he is not/does not feel sad in light of this fact

---

[20]Note that, once again, this contrast involves reason-requests concerning direct perception, not reasons requests concerning aspectperception. Thus, Poellner's (2016) reply to the observation concerning justificatory reasons (see n. 19) is of no help here either. For the disanalogy with respect to aspect perception, cf. section 4 of this chapter.

Crucially, these sentences seem semantically anomalous. Accordingly, they indicate that the attribution of a target to an emotion or its felt aspect entails that this target constitutes a motivating reason for it. As these examples suggest, to conceive of an emotional feeling as directed is to recognize it a response to its target.[21]

This take on the directedness of emotional feeling adds further support to the claim that it differs from perception in respect of intentionality. As already noted, perceptions are not responses in the sense relevant here. In line with the observation that the question "why do you perceive x?" makes no sense as an enquiry about motivating reasons, it also makes no sense to say that we enjoy perceptions in light of or on occasion of their objects.[22] While it is true that when Maria feels afraid of the dog, she has a particular feeling in light or on occasion of the dog, it is not true that when Maria has a vivid perception of the landscape, she has a perception in light or on occasion of the landscape. Although we can think of her perception as caused by the landscape, it is not a response to it in the here relevant sense.

Accordingly, emotional feeling and perception seem to relate to their objects in different ways. Note that this difference holds with respect to any form of impression or presentation. While we may give causal explanations of these phenomena, there is nothing *in light of* which one has impressions or is being 'appeared to' in some way. Correspondingly, what one has an impression of is never a reason for which one has the

---

[21] In a similar vein, Dietz (2018) argues that the propositional content of factive emotions (ascribed by means of "*S V*s that *p*") is a motivating reason for them. It seems to me that the basic point is not restricted to factive emotions. For a clear case in hand, consider this variant of the second example: "Maria is/feels afraid that the motorbike will hit her, but not because this prospect appears in any way threatening to her". This sentence, too, is anomalous. Cf. also Müller (2017, 288, n. 19). An intimate connection between targets and motivating reasons is recognized also by Kenny in his discussion of objects and causes of an emotion (cf. 2003 [1963], 52ff.) as well as by Donnellan (1971). Donnellan distinguishes between the objects of emotions and motivating reasons for them (what he calls "producers"). I take it that Donnellan is right about this distinction insofar as it is never the target of an emotion *simpliciter* that constitutes a reason for which it is felt, but a specific aspect of it. Cf. the discussion in the main text below.

[22] The responsive character of emotions and their felt aspects also distinguishes them from reflex-like behaviours and reactive sensations. This seems to me not to be fully appreciated by Zamuner (2015), who argues that that emotions are psychological reactions, which bear important similarities with reactive bodily sensations. Although some of what Zamuner says implies that he sees emotions as having motivating reasons, he does not draw a sufficiently clear distinction between responses and mere bodily reactions.

impression. It is worth stressing, moreover, that in fact no view of emotion or emotional feeling as apprehending or registering aspects of the world is able to acknowledge its responsive character (cf. also Mulligan 2010b, 485; Müller 2017, 285f.).[23] Note that, as a request for motivating reasons, the question "why do you apprehend/register *x*?" is just as meaningless. The same goes for the corresponding questions involving cognate verbs such as "grasp", "discover", "detect", "(come to) be aware of", "know". Relatedly, what we apprehend or register is not something to which the apprehending or registering is a response and hence at which it is directed (cf. also Müller 2019, section 1.1).

The difference which I have highlighted here is related to an observation that is sometimes expressed by saying that emotions, but not perceptions, have a 'cognitive basis' (cf. Deonna and Teroni 2012, 69; 2014, 24f.). That is, in order to have an emotion or emotional feeling directed at something one must have some prior awareness of it. Perception, in contrast, seems to be a self-standing intentional phenomenon. Thus, to be/feel glad about the scene, the scene must have been perceived by Peter. In contrast, his perception of the scene itself does not seem to be dependent on any further cognitive state. As far as I can see, this difference is a direct consequence of the disanalogy I have pointed out. If it is correct that emotions and emotional feelings are directed at things as responses to them, then it follows that they require prior awareness of their target. That is, the dog can be a reason for which Maria is afraid only if she has apprehended and thus come to be aware of it. More generally, aspects of a situation can be reasons for which someone acts (thinks, feels etc.) in some way only if they are within her cognitive ken. (To be precise, in case the motivating reason is not an actual, but illusory, aspect of the situation, she responds to what she merely seems to be aware of or, put differently, to the object of her awareness *as of* the situation.) Thus, it is no surprise that, in contrast to perceptions, emotions and their felt aspects have a cognitive basis. This

---

[23] I read Deonna and Teroni (2012, 2014, 2015) as defending a view according to which emotions, or their felt aspects in particular, apprehend value without being assimilated to perception. Cf. also Sect. 1.1 in Chapter 2, n. 8. I discuss their view in Sect. 3 in Chapter 4.

difference is underwritten by the fact they are responses to their target while perceptions are not responses to their object.[24]

In order to make explicit an additional, related difficulty with AR, I would like to add one further detail to the picture that has so far emerged of emotional feeling. We can refine this picture so as to show it to be in tension with AR in another important respect by considering more closely what precisely it is about their target that makes emotional feelings responsive to it. A closer look at explanatory practice suggests that the felt dimension of an emotion is in fact responsive to just those properties which it is supposed to disclose according to AR. More precisely, the reasons for which we have emotional feelings always include an apparent exemplification of the corresponding formal object by their target. This observation provides the basis for a further objection against AR.[25]

Considerations on ordinary ascriptions of emotions and their felt aspects very similar to the ones presented above suggest that in ascribing an emotion or emotional feeling we implicitly conceive of it as a response to an appearance of its formal object.[26]

*Peter is/feels glad about the scene, though he is not/does not feel glad because the scene appears to have any positive import to him whatsoever

---

[24]Tappolet (2016, 30) argues that the difference in terms of cognitive base is compatible with emotion being a form of presentation (or, as she calls it, "openness"). However, Tappolet is not alive to the fact that the cognitive basis of an emotion is an enabling condition for it to be directed as a response to something. Qua enabling condition of emotional directedness, it is incompatible with the proposed analogy between emotion and perception because the directedness of emotions and their felt aspects makes them intelligible as a mode of intentionality fundamentally different from presentation.

Poellner (2016, 275ff.) has questioned the disanalogy in respect of cognitive basis by noting that perceptions of higher-order properties (which include values) are dependent on certain cognitions, too. That is, in order for someone to perceive a higher-order property some of the subtending lower-level properties must have registered with her. However, perceptions of higher-order properties are not responses to the subtending lower-level properties. Thus, whatever cognitions are required of the latter for the perception of the former to occur, they do not provide access to motivating reasons.

[25]The objection is found also in Mulligan (2004, 216f., 218f.; 2010a, 233f.; 2010b, 485) and Teroni (2007, 405). I here develop it in what seems to me to be the most transparent way. Cf. also Müller (2017, section 3.2; 2019, section 1.1).

[26]In the following examples, I use 'because' rather than 'in light of' or 'on occasion of' to specify motivating reasons in order to reduce syntactic complexity. Note that they can all be paraphrased by using these latter locutions.

*Maria is/feels afraid of the approaching motorbike, though she is not/does not feel afraid because the motorbike appears even remotely threatening to her

*George is/feels sad that the show has closed, though he is not/does not feel sad because its closure appears to him as a loss of any sort

These sentences, too, seem semantically anomalous. They indicate that the attribution of a target to an emotion or emotional feeling entails that there is a specific evaluative respect in which its target appears and which constitutes a motivating reason for that emotion or feeling.[27] Accordingly, in conceiving of an emotional feeling as directed we conceive of it as a response to the corresponding formal object.[28]

Now, the claim that emotions are responses to (dis)value is not uncontroversial. For example, taking some inspiration from Scheler (1973 [1913–1916]) and Voigtländer (1910, 111), Vendrell Ferran (2008, 212) denies that this is true of what she calls "personality emotions" (cf. also ibid., 171). These are thought to disclose certain response-dependent properties (which she distinguishes from values) and include religious emotions, such as beatitude, existential emotions, such as existential envy, but also admiration, love and hatred.[29] If Vendrell Ferran is right, there are emotional feelings that are not felt in light of their formal object. There is a question here whether all of her examples should be classed as bona fide emotions. For example, I would discount beatitude since it does not seem to me to be directed at anything: we are not blissful at, of, about, for or over anything (cf. also Sect. 1.2 in Chapter 2, n. 15). It seems clear, though, that not all of them can be discounted in this way. As far as I can see, however, regarding those cases which are widely accepted to be emo-

---

[27] I should stress that the point here is not merely that one must conceive of the subject of an emotion or emotional feeling as construing its target in a particular evaluative way if the emotion or feeling is to be intelligibly ascribable to her. Its intelligibility requires also that one think of this evaluative respect as a *reason for which* she has it.

[28] I take it that this is in line with de Sousa's (2011, 72) and Mulligan's (2010b, 485) considerations of the connection between emotions and formal objects, though they do not explicitly argue for the value responsive character of emotion in this way.

[29] She calls them "personality emotions" since the disclosure of these properties (e.g. hatefulness, lovability) is conceived as being in a certain sense contingent on the individual having them.

tions, Vendrell Ferran's claim is mistaken. Thus, the following ascriptions seem to me just as anomalous:

*Ned is/feels envious of Jerry's very persona, though he is not/does not feel envious because Jerry's persona strikes Ned as valuable in any respect
*George admires/feels admiration towards Peter, though he does not admire/feel admiration towards Peter because Peter appears excellent to him in any way
*Sally loves/feels love for James, though she does not love/feel love for James because James appears appealing or attractive to her at all
*Edward is/feels hateful towards Lucy, though he is not/does not feel hateful because she appears in the least evil or base to him

Here, too, I would maintain, we have ascriptions of emotions/emotional feelings which are unintelligible and thus indicate that existential envy, admiration, love, hatred, and the corresponding feelings, are responses to apparent exemplifications of their formal object. Indeed, Vendrell Ferran (2008, 212) herself seems to allow that we love another because of certain of her qualities, but denies that love is a response to these. I think this is inconsistent. If those qualities are reasons for which we love someone, then our love is a response to them. Moreover, in light of my above remarks on responses and apprehension, I take the fact that these emotions/emotional feelings are directed as responses to their target to be incompatible with the view that they apprehend or disclose response-dependent properties.[30]

If it is true that emotional feelings are always responses to their formal object, this raises a further problem for AR because, in favourable circumstances, the evaluative appearance to which an emotional feeling is a response already does the epistemic work which AR accords to emotional

---

[30] I am similarly unconvinced by a further objection by Zamuner (2015, 35f.) who argues on empirical grounds that emotions are not necessarily reactions to evaluations. His argument is aimed against the idea that some evaluative state is a necessary condition for the occurrence of emotion, as the above examples suggest. However, as he himself notes (ibid., 36, n. 28), these empirical considerations only tell against the claim that emotions necessarily require conceptual evaluations. Note that the above examples are deliberately framed in terms of appearance rather than belief. There is no supposition that the respective evaluative state is conceptual. Cf. also Chapter 5. I respond to a further possible concern with this picture, raised by Teroni (2007) and Deonna and Teroni (2012, chapter 8), in my (2017, 289, n. 21).

feeling. More specifically, under certain conditions this appearance is a case of actually apprehending a value and thus constitutes awareness of value. Now, crucially the evaluative appearance to which an emotional feeling is a response is also (at least in part) what brings about the feeling. Hence, the appearance temporally precedes the feeling. Accordingly, in such cases, the respective value is apprehended *prior to* the feeling. But this means that the feeling does not apprehend or disclose this value: one cannot apprehend what one has already apprehended. This is because it is not possible to bring within someone's cognitive ken what is already within it. We can make this line of thought more precise as follows (cf. Müller 2017, 289ff.):

1. Necessarily, the felt aspect of S's emotion responds to how its target x evaluatively appears to S.
2. Where S's emotional feeling towards x is a response to how x appears to S, the appearance temporally precedes S's feeling.
3. In some cases, the prior appearance constitutes an apprehension of the value of x; in the other cases, it constitutes a mere apprehension as of the value of x.
4. When S's emotional feeling responds to an appearance which apprehends the value of x, S apprehends this value prior to S's feeling.
5. It is not possible for S to apprehend what S has already apprehended.
6. When S's emotional feeling is responsive to an appearance which apprehends the value of x, S's feeling does not apprehend the value of x.

This line of thought considerably restricts the possibility for emotional feelings to play the epistemic role assigned to them by AR: emotional feelings cannot be disclosive of value when they are at the same time based on awareness of value. Of course, not all emotional feelings are based on actual awareness of value. There are cases where the evaluative appearance is non-veridical. However, in these cases, there is no value to be apprehended by the feeling in the first place. Thus, such cases do not constitute instances of emotional feeling that apprehend value either.[31]

---

[31] I have here set aside a further, unusual case where the evaluative appearance is accidentally veridical. As I argue in my (2017, 291f.), in this case the emotion does not provide epistemic access to value either.

If these remarks are correct, it follows that the observation that emotional feelings are directed falsifies AR. If for them to be directed implies that they are responses to apparent value, then emotional feelings do not present or otherwise apprehend value. Rather, emotions are consequent upon an apprehension as of value. We can elaborate the positive picture of the connection between emotional feeling and value that has emerged as follows (cf. Müller 2017, 290, 292).[32] All emotional feelings are responses to an appearance of their formal object. Where this appearance constitutes awareness of an actual exemplification of their formal object, we can also say that the feeling is a response to this exemplification itself: it is a response to what we are aware of. In this case, it is permissible not only to say that the subject of the emotion feels some way towards a given object because that object appears valuable or disvaluable in some respect, but also that she feels that way because it *is* valuable or disvaluable in this respect (or, alternatively, that she feels that way in light of its (dis)value). In the other cases, emotional feelings are responses to value appearances which constitute mere awareness as of an exemplification of their formal object. In these cases, we are not aware of an actual exemplification of the formal object. Here, the reason for which we have the feeling is its mere apparent exemplification.

It is interesting that philosophers sympathetic to AR occasionally seem to endorse the idea of an emotional value response. For example, Helm (2001, chapters 2 and 3; 2002, 2009) speaks of emotional feelings as "responses to import". In a similar vein, some of Poellner's (2016, 269f.) remarks suggest that he takes the fact that emotions are responses to their targets qua (dis)valuable to be perfectly compatible with (or even support) the claim that they are (quasi-)perceptual experiences of value. Poellner in fact seems to suppose that the value responsive phenomenology of emotion helps to defuse the charge that the phenomenology of emotion is very different from the phenomenology of perception.[33] Now, there is

---

[32]This picture is congenial to the disjunctive view of reasons for action offered by Hornsby (2008) and McDowell (2013). Mulligan's (2007, 2010b) considerations on emotional responses suggest a picture on these lines, too.

[33]He refers to the charge as raised by Deonna and Teroni (2015, 306). To be precise, Poellner's main goal in this passage to is to defend the perceptual model against another charge by Deonna and Teroni, according to which the intentional content of emotion is not evaluative. He does not seem to

of course a question as to how precisely the use of "response" is to be interpreted in these cases. If what I have argued in this section is correct, then emotions and the involved feelings are not responses to value in a mere causal sense, but rather in the sense connected to motivating reasons. Helm and Poellner do not seem to fully appreciate that emotions and their felt aspects are value responses in this latter sense and thus are involved with value in a way that is fundamentally different from the link between perceptions and their objects. As I have stressed in this section, there are several reasons to suppose that this form of involvement with value distinguishes them from perceptions or any other forms of apprehension of value.[34]

Note, moreover, that it is not an option for proponents of AR to claim that the value appearance which precedes an emotion or emotional feeling somehow comes to form part of it. This view does not help vindicate the idea that values are registered or apprehended by emotional feelings since, as I explained, as long as the feeling is subsequent to the appearance, exemplifications of the corresponding formal object will already have been apprehended when the feeling occurs. Moreover, one should not forget that the role of the value appearance is to make available a reason for which we have the feeling. Mental states that make available reasons for which we act (think, feel etc.) are generally distinct from what they provide a reason for. When S believes that x is F for the reason that x looks F, the perceptual experience which makes available the reason for which S holds this belief is not a constitutive part of S's belief. The analogous point holds for the value appearances on which emotions and emotional feelings depend as responses to apparent value. That is, neither the cognitive basis nor the value appearance which provides the evaluative aspect under which

---

be aware, though, that an adequate understanding of the responsive character of emotion precisely tells against them having a perception-like phenomenology. Indeed, it also tells against them having evaluative content. Cf. my (2017). I will not take up the issue about content here, though.

[34] Helm might agree that as value responses emotional feelings differ from perceptions. At any rate, he distinguishes them from perceptions in respect of involving assent. Cf. (2001, 45f., 64ff.). However, as I read him, he wants to hold on to the idea that they are also impressions of value. This is incompatible with their responsive character.

they are directed at something are constitutive parts of them (cf. Mulligan 2010b, 488).[35]

4 A Possible Concern: Affectivity and Directedness

It can perhaps seem that the way in which I have contrasted emotional feelings and impressions up to this point conflicts with certain further intuitions we have about the respective phenomena. To begin with, some might think that as a sense of being touched or affected, emotional feeling is a way of being receptive to the world and, thus, a form of impression after all.[36] Is there a tension between the claim that emotional feeling is a matter of being affected and the claim that it is directed and hence responsive in the way I have indicated?

As far as I can see, this concern misconceives the characterization of emotional feeling that I have provided. The affectation essential to emotion must be sharply distinguished from sensory affectation or any other form of impression. Emotional affectation is itself directed and responsive in the sense I have been concerned with. That is, to suppose of someone that she is moved or affected by something in the way characteristic of a particular emotion is to think of her as having a corresponding emotional feeling directed at that thing. Consider, for example, what it means to say of someone that she is gladdened or frightened by something. In the first instance, we thereby characterize her as being positively or negatively affected or touched by something. But for her to be positively (negatively) affected or touched by something in these cases is for her to feel some way *in light of* that thing. That is, it is for her to feel good (bad) or be (dis)pleased *about* it.

---

[35] While agreeing that the value awareness on which an emotion depends qua value response is not a constitutive part of it, Mulligan supposes that the cognitive basis of an emotion is. Cf. (ibid., 476). However, in providing access to the target, the cognitive basis also directly contributes to making available a reason for which one has an emotion and therefore ought to be recognized as a distinct mental state as well.

[36] Some authors who distinguish between emotion and what they call "being affected" (cf. Sect. 1 in Chapter 2) suppose that only the former is a response, while the latter is more akin to perception. Cf. von Hildebrand (1953, 209).

It is important here to appreciate that the preposition "by" in connection with these uses of "affected by" or "touched by" is not to be interpreted as indicating a mere cause. Rather, it specifies what the respective feeling is responsive to. Thus, ascriptions of the form "*S* is affected/touched/moved by *x*" can be paraphrased as "*S* is affected/touched/moved in light of *x*". Note also that, while it is perhaps less common to ask "Why are you affected by *x*?" and to thereby enquire about the reason for which someone has a certain emotional feeling, the question certainly makes good sense as an enquiry of this sort. We clearly do ask the question "Why are you touched/moved by *x*?" in this vein: "Why are you touched by his innocuous remark?"—"Because it was pretty offensive." "Why are you moved by this piece of art?"—"Because it is beautiful." In asking these questions, we enquire about motivating reasons. The same is true of "Why are you affected by *x*?": "Why are you affected by his silly remark?"—"Because it was pretty offensive.", "Because he knows how to be mean." These observations suggest that in characterizing emotional feelings as ways of being affected, we do not characterize them as a type of impression, but as responses.[37]

While there is thus no obvious tension between the way in which I have here juxtaposed emotional feeling and presentation and the intuition that emotional feeling is a form of affectation, one might think that my considerations are yet in tension with a certain intuition we have regarding a particular form of presentation. That is, it can seem that there is a kind of impression to which proponents of AR sometimes appeal in developing their view, which allows for descriptions under which it is amenable to the same types of reason-enquiry as emotions and their felt aspects. Consider

---

[37] There is more to be said about the relation between the affective aspect of emotions and the sense in which they are directed and responsive. Von Hildebrand (1969a [1916], 9, n. 1, 11, 13; 1953, 196f., 209) takes emotions qua directed to be a form of activity (or, as he calls it, spontaneity), which contrasts with the receptivity of perception and other cognitive acts. Cf. also Müller (2019, section 1.1). I hope to elaborate on this point in future work in the context of a more thorough examination of the question in which sense emotions can be said to be passive. Note that the dissimilarity I have highlighted between emotional feeling and perception in this chapter does not necessarily undermine the idea that both perception and emotion are in a certain sense passive. Thinking of emotions and their felt aspects as directed is compatible with them being passive in the sense of being beyond our voluntary control. Yet emotional passivity is different from perceptual passivity in that it is not a matter of (quasi-)perceptually registering aspects of the world.

familiar cases of aspectual impression.[38] In seeing Jastrow's duck-rabbit picture as a duck, one has an impression of a certain feature of the image (its 'duckiness'). At the same time one can ask someone enjoying this impression "Why do you see the figure as a duck?" This question can be read as a request for a motivating reason. One is enquiring about the perceiver's reason for seeing the figure in this way. Note that someone who was instructed to see the figure as a duck and arrives at the corresponding impression (at least partly) through an effort of will, might intelligibly respond: "Because you asked me to." She thereby seems to make her impression intelligible as a response to the interlocutor's request. Perhaps even features of the object of the impression (the image) can be cited as motivating reasons in this context. It does not seem outlandish to suppose that "Because this blotch looks very much like a beak." is an intelligible answer to an enquiry of this sort. If this is correct, it can seem that, in contrast to what I said, some forms of presentation can be responses, even responses to aspects of their object.

We can see that this line of thought rests on a confusion once we draw a distinction between aspectual impressions and their cognitive preconditions. In order to enjoy an impression of the figure's 'duckiness' one must experience it against the background of a certain visual acquaintance with ducks. In Roberts' (2003, 2013) terms, one must *construe* the figure in terms of something else (e.g. a certain visual image of a duck). It is by bringing to bear certain (broadly speaking) cognitive resources on one's primary visual awareness of the figure that it visually appears in this way. The terms "see *x* as *F*" and "perceive *x* as *F*" are ambiguous between the act of *construing* an object in a given way and the constru*al*, the impression of a certain aspect one obtains in so construing it.[39] For example, in asking

---

[38] For versions of AR that assimilate emotional feeling to aspectual impressions, cf. Roberts (2003, 2013), Döring (2004, chapters 8 and 9), and Slaby (2008, chapter 9). Perhaps Helm's (2001, chapter 2) view can be read in this way, too. In this connection, cf. also Müller (2011). Similarly, on the interpretation of Scheler's and Sartre's view of emotion, which Poellner (2016) propounds, some emotions are (quasi-)perceptual experiences of the values of things *as such*, i.e. as the values they are. As he characterizes them, these emotions disclose or present values in virtue of having a specific felt aspect. As indicated before (n. 19), Poellner also adverts to 'perceiving as' in defending his view.

[39] Roberts himself does not clearly draw this distinction. He seems to suppose (mistakenly) that it is possible for impressions themselves to be had for reasons. Cf. his account of what he calls "analytic causes" in (2003, chapter 2, section 6).

someone to see Jastrow's figure as a duck, one is asking her to construe it in a certain way; one does not ask her to be presented with a certain aspect or to be 'appeared to' in a certain way. This distinction is crucial to understanding requests for reasons in this context. When the question "Why are you seeing the figure as a duck?" asks for the perceiver's reason for seeing the figure in a particular way, the reason requested is her reason for constru*ing* the figure in a specific way, not for the corresponding impression. It is just as misleading to enquire about someone's reasons for enjoying an impression of a figure's ducky shape as it is to enquire about someone's reasons for enjoying impressions of colour.

What I have said in this chapter about emotional feelings as responses has direct implications for an adequate account of the intelligibility conditions of emotion. The observation that we must conceive of the way someone emotionally feels towards something as responsive to an apparent exemplification of its formal object in order for her feeling to be intelligible imposes a constraint on the intelligibility of her emotion. In this respect, it seems to directly bear on an issue I raised in explicating the notion of the formal object in Sect. 2.1, Chapter 2. In the final section, I briefly return to this issue to further refine the account of formal objects presented there and note some further implications of my remarks on the responsiveness of emotional feeling.

5 Implications for the Significance and Structure of Formal Objects

What I have said about the responsive character of emotional feeling allows us to refine our account of the significance of the formal objects of emotions as follows. It seems that the role of formal objects with respect to the intelligibility conditions of emotions is first and foremost that of providing a constraint on what emotions are responsive to. In other words, the formal object of a given emotion type constitutes the reason for which instances of that emotion must be enjoyed if they are to be intelligible as such.[40] It specifies what we necessarily have 'in view' in enjoying instances of that emotion.

This constraint on the reasons for which we have emotions is very similar to the intelligibility requirement, as I have formulated it in Sect. 2.1, Chapter 2. I there noted that for an emotion to be intelligible as such, its subject must apprehend its particular object as exemplifying its formal object or as having features suitably intimately related to it. Note, though, that this constraint entails a stronger requirement: the particular object must be apprehended as exemplifying the formal object itself. Thus, we can now see that accounts of the intelligibility conditions of emotion that merely require the subject of an emotion to apprehend its particular object as having features that are intimately related to, but distinct from, its formal object are mistaken and further qualify the account of emotional intelligibility given in Sect. 2.1, Chapter 2 in terms of this stronger requirement.[41]

Before I conclude this chapter, I would like to note that my considerations on the responsiveness of emotional feeling in the last section do not only have consequences for an appropriate understanding of the significance of formal objects. They also lend further support to the specific view of their structure, which I sketched at the end of the first chapter. This view seems to sit quite well with the claim that emotions are responses to their formal objects. From a first-person point of view, it seems plausible to suppose that what we ultimately respond to in enjoying emotions is the way in which things seem positively or negatively relevant to something as an object of concern. Intuitively, what you have in view in fearing something is always its apparent potential to harm something *qua significant to you*—you are emotionally responsive to a specific type of badness, which consists in its negative relevance to or incongruence with a particular care or attachment. Likewise, what motivates our anger at someone is always

---

[40]This closely relates to de Sousa's (2011, 72) claim that the "most trivial possible answer possible to the question 'Why do you S O?' for state S and object O, yields the FO [formal object, JMM]." Although this is not explicit in what he says, I take it that Mulligan (2010b, 485) would agree with this.

[41]One might think that there are additional consequences of the idea that emotions are value responses for an adequate understanding of the roles of formal objects. I here lack the space to further expand on this. In my (2017, section 4.2), I show that this idea has ramifications also for the notion of emotional fittingness.

how their conduct purportedly offends against and thus seems negatively relevant to something *qua object of our concern*. Similarly, when you are glad to have completed your goals for the day, you are responsive to the positive relevance of their completion for your corresponding desire. You are responsive to goodness in the sense of congruence with this desire.

I think it is helpful in this context to, once again, consider ordinary emotional experience somewhat more closely. Rather than directly focusing on the responsive character of emotion, it may in fact be more helpful to look instead at how situations are apprehended immediately prior to emotion. Thus, imagine a situation in which you receive a condescending look from a colleague, but initially withhold anger. As you experience your colleague's look, it presents itself as something that *calls*, as we would say, for a certain response. It is, experientially speaking, characterized in part by a certain solicitation or demand to feel a particular way—to feel angry.[42] Moreover, and crucially, this solicitation possesses a certain authority. There is *normative* pressure to feel that way, where the normativity of this pressure is (in part) derivative of your *caring about* being treated in a respectful and dignified way. More precisely, it derives from the way in which your colleague's look conflicts with something you are invested into: you experience this demand inasmuch as you sense that it is *in tension with your concerns*. It is this negative bearing on your cares that you ultimately have 'in view' as you are getting emotionally involved, what you respond to when you ultimately get angry at the offender.

Considerations along these lines suggest that a phenomenologically adequate account of emotions as responses to their formal objects should conceive of formal objects as having the relational structure I alluded to in Sect. 2.2, Chapter 2. The axiological properties we respond to in emotion, it seems, are relational properties, whose axiological character is to be

---

[42] Cf. Scheler (1973 [1913–1916], 258f.), von Hildebrand (1953, 38f., 199f., chapter 18) on the idea that axiological properties call for or solicit emotional responses. Cf. also Müller (2019, section 2.2). Von Hildebrand distinguishes different kinds of solicitation in connection with different species of significance. He would presumably disagree with my characterization of the pressure to feel angry in the above example. As he supposes, where significance is derivative of one's interests and concerns, it 'tempts' or 'invites' certain responses, but does not 'demand' them in the strict sense of the term. I disagree with him on this point. It seems to me that the solicitations connected with our grasp of the bearing of things on our concerns can be genuine 'demands'. In fact, it seems that it is precisely their link to our concerns to which they owe their deontic force in this case.

understood in terms of the (un)favourable bearing of something on our concerns. This seems to cohere nicely also with the view of emotional feeling I sketched in Sect. 1.2, Chapter 2 and which will be further elaborated in the subsequent chapter: things affect us personally—we are moved as subject of particular cares and concerns—in light of their significance to us as subjects of those concerns. That we are personally affected by something makes sense in view of the way it bears on our personal investments.

Now, as I noted at the end of my discussion of formal objects in Sect. 2.2, Chapter 2, some philosophers complain that a conception of formal objects as essentially relative to individual cares and concerns is too subjectivist to provide sufficiently robust appropriateness conditions for emotion. One might maintain that ordinary critical practice clearly looks beyond the question of whether or not the particular object of someone's emotion actually bears on her concerns in assessing whether or not it is appropriate (cf. Slaby 2008, chapter 8, esp. 8.4).[43]

It seems to me that, in light of my further considerations on the responsive character of emotion, the demand for formal objects to provide more robust conditions of appropriateness that are independent of an individual evaluative perspective should be rejected. Although it is no doubt correct that our critical assessments of emotion are not exhausted by considerations on the bearing of things relative to individual concerns, it is important not to lose sight of the fact that such considerations do provide an important dimension of our normative appraisal of them. There is a clear sense in which your fear of the impending rain is fitting if the rain has the potential to harm something you care about and unfitting if it does not. This is important inasmuch as it suggests that there is a question here as to which of several standards for the critical assessment of emotions which are invoked in ordinary critical practice we ought to be sensitive to in formulating an account of formal objects. If, as I have suggested above, it is plausible to suppose that the axiological properties we are responsive

---

[43] Von Hildebrand (1969a [1916], 37ff.; 1953, chapter 18) maintains on different grounds that we are often emotionally responsive to values that are independent of our concerns. Cf. also Müller (2019, section 2.1). Though his considerations raise a further substantive issue, I will here have to postpone detailed treatment of it. While I agree that e.g. in admiration it does not seem to us that we are responsive to significance that is relative to our interests, I would maintain that we are nonetheless ultimately responsive to excellence qua exemplification of what we value. Cf. also Roberts (2003, 264f.) on the concern for excellence involved in admiration.

to in emotion are species of significance relative to our concerns, considerations of coherence suggest opting for a standard which refers to this type of property, too. Formal objects impose both a constraint on the intelligibility of emotions and on their appropriateness. If it is true that what we are emotionally responsive to and what makes our emotion intelligible is a concern-relative type of significance and there is also standard of fittingness which invokes that property, I take it we have rather strong reason to suppose that this is the relevant standard. It is moreover worth stressing that in recognizing formal objects as providing conditions of fittingness that are relative to an individual's concerns, we do not have to deny that ordinary critical practice recognizes further, more objective standards of propriety. What is denied is only that these are specified by the formal object of an emotion. In what follows, I shall suppose that the formal objects of emotions are relational properties, whose axiological character consists in the (un)favourable bearing of something on our concerns.

6 Conclusion

My principal aim in this chapter was to show that the currently most prominent intentionalist view of emotional feeling is in serious tension with our ordinary conception of emotion. After providing some further elaboration on AR and its central, phenomenological motivation, I argued that, in contrast to what its proponents assume, the manifest image of occurrent emotion displays emotional feeling as an intentional mode that is fundamentally different from presentation. As I proposed, ordinary experience and discourse represent emotional feeling as feeling towards. On this picture, emotional affectivity is *directed* in a way that contrasts with the mode of intentionality constituted by impressions or presentations. I elaborated my account of the distinctness of feeling towards from presentation in terms of their connection to reasons, arguing that feeling towards, but not presentation, is essentially responsive to features of its object, which necessarily include apparent exemplifications of the corresponding formal object. I claimed that this, too, is incompatible with the significance assigned by AR to emotional feeling: emotional feeling cannot be simultaneously responsive to and disclosive of value.

I take these considerations to provide strong grounds to reject AR. To the extent that we are interested in illuminating emotional feeling and its significance in a way that is faithful to our ordinary conception of emotion, AR is clearly deficient. The manifest image of emotion does not support, but in fact undermines AR. While it is coherent with AR to the extent that it conceives of emotional feeling as intentional, it conceives of it as an intentional occurrence that could not be more different from presentations of value.

In the following chapter, I expand on the account of emotional feeling I have offered in this chapter. As will become clear, the picture of emotional feeling that I have here opposed to AR does not merely show that AR misrepresents the significance of emotional feeling, but at the same time supports an alternative, more appropriate, intentionalist view. According this view, emotional feeling is a specific form of position-taking rather than 'cognizance-taking'. Some of what I have said in this chapter has already alluded to this account of the significance of emotional feeling. But there is more to be said by way of laying it out properly.

As a final remark, I would like to point out that my discussion in this chapter has implications for a question that is not directly in the focus of this inquiry, but possesses significance within the broader context of the debate I am concerned with. This is the question regarding the ontological connection between occurrent emotion and emotional feeling. As I noted in the Introduction, according to a conception that was prominent in the second half of the twentieth century, emotions are comprised of several components, including but not limited to feeling. Here, it was generally supposed that several central aspects of occurrent emotion, in particular their directedness, their intimate link to cognition and their conditions of fittingness, require elucidation in terms of a dimension separate from their felt aspects. The considerations of this chapter cast strong doubt on this. It seems plausible to suppose that emotions take objects and are intimately related to cognitions in virtue of involving feelings towards. The same seems true of their conditions of fittingness. The way we feel towards a given object in occurrent emotion is subject to fittingness conditions, too, indeed to just those we associate with emotions: we think it (un)fitting for someone to feel afraid of or sad about something depending on whether the object of her feeling exemplifies the formal object of the corresponding emotion. In light of this, it seems that those features traditionally associated with occurrent emotions are really features of their felt aspects. And this makes it seem fairly compelling to question that emotion and emotional feeling are distinct occurrences.

What I say in the next chapter might be thought to provide additional reason to identify the two. In developing the idea that emotional feelings are position-takings, they are shown to display a kind of internal complexity that might be thought to capture much of the complexity we ordinarily associate with occurrent emotion. However, while I believe that the account of emotional feeling I am elaborating provides strong grounds to identify occurrent emotions and their felt aspects, I nonetheless wish to stay neutral on this issue. Some theorists suppose that ordinary experience shows that occurrences of paradigm emotions comprise feeling towards as well as additional intentional occurrences (cf. e.g. Goldie 2000, chapter 1; 2002; 2009). As a more thorough assessment of this type of component view would here lead us too far afield, I shall leave the question of the ontological connection between occurrent emotion and emotional feeling open. Regardless of how this question is to be settled, my discussion should however leave little doubt that whatever else we might want to think of as part of emotion, our sense of being affected is clearly at the heart of it.

References

Alvarez, Maria. 2010. *Kinds of reasons*. Oxford: Oxford University Press.
Bittner, Rüdiger. 2001. *Doing things for reasons*. Oxford: Oxford University Press.
Brady, Michael. 2007. Recalcitrant emotions and visual illusions. *American Philosophical Quarterly* 44: 273–284.
Brady, Michael. 2011. Emotions, perceptions, and reasons. In *Morality and the emotions*, ed. Carla Bagnoli, 135–149. New York: Oxford University Press.
Brady, Michael. 2013. *Emotional insight*. Oxford: Oxford University Press.
Chudnoff, Elijah. 2012. Presentational phenomenology. In *Consciousness and subjectivity*, ed. Sofia Miguens and Gerhard Preyer, 51–72. Frankfurt am Main: Ontos.
Deonna, Julien, and Fabrice Teroni. 2008. *Qu'est-ce qu'une émotion?* Paris: Vrin.

Deonna, Julien, and Fabrice Teroni. 2012. *The emotions*. London: Routledge.
Deonna, Julien, and Fabrice Teroni. 2014. In what sense are emotions evaluations? In *Emotion and value*, ed. Sabine Roeser and Cain Todd, 15–31. Oxford: Oxford University Press.
Deonna, Julien, and Fabrice Teroni. 2015. Emotions as attitudes. *Dialectica* 69 (3): 293–311.
de Sousa, Ronald. 2011. *Emotional truth*. Oxford: Oxford University Press.
Dietz, Christina. 2018. Reasons and factive emotions. *Philosophical Studies* 175 (7): 1681–1691.
Dokic, Jerôme and Stéphane Lemaire. 2013. Are emotions perceptions of value? *Canadian Journal of Philosophy* 43(2): 227–247.
Donnellan, Keith. 1971. Causes, objects and producers of emotion. *Journal of Philosophy* 67: 947–950.
Döring, Sabine. 2004. *Gründe und Gefühle*. Habilitationsschrift [Second book]. Duisburg-Essen University.
Findlay, John N. 1935. Emotional presentation. *Australasian Journal of Philosophy* 13 (2): 111–121.
Goldie, Peter. 2000. *The emotions*. Oxford: Clarendon Press.
Goldie, Peter. 2002. Emotion, feeling and intentionality. *Phenomenology and the Cognitive Sciences* 1 (3): 235–254.
Goldie, Peter. 2009. Getting feelings into emotional experience in the right way. *Emotion Review* 1 (3): 232–239.
Heidegger, Martin 1962. *Being and time,* trans. J. Macquarie and E. Robinson. New York: Harper & Row. Original edition: Heidegger, Martin. 1927. *Sein und Zeit*. Tübingen: Max Niemeyer.
Helm, Bennett. 2001. *Emotional reason*. Cambridge: Cambridge University Press.
Helm, Bennett. 2002. Felt evaluations: A theory of pleasure and pain. *American Philosophical Quarterly* 39 (1): 13–30.
Helm, Bennett. 2009. Emotions as evaluative feelings. *Emotion Review* 1 (3): 248–255.
Hornsby, Jennifer. 2008. A disjunctive conception of acting for reasons. In *Disjunctivism,* ed. Adrian Haddock and Fiona MacPherson, 244–261. Oxford: Oxford University Press.
Husserl, Edmund. 1988. *Vorlesungen über Ethik und Wertlehre 1908–1914*. Dordrecht: Kluwer.
Husserl, Edmund. 1989. *Ideas pertaining to a pure phenomenology and to a phenomenological philosophy: Second book studies in the phenomenology of constitution,* trans. R. Rojcewicz and A. Schuwer. Dordrecht: Kluwer. Original edition:

Husserl, Edmund. 1952. *Ideen zu einer reinen Phänomenologie und phänomenologischen Philosophie. Zweites Buch: Phänomenologische Untersuchungen zur Konstitution*. Den Haag: Martinus Nijhoff.

Kenny, Anthony. 2003. *Action, emotion and will*, 2nd ed. London: Routledge and Kegan Paul (Original edition 1963).

McDowell, John. 1996. *Mind and world*, 2nd ed. Cambridge, MA: Harvard University Press.

McDowell, J. 2013. Acting in the light of a fact. In *Thinking about reasons*, ed. David Bakhurst, Margeret O. Little, and Brad Hooker, 13–28. Oxford: Oxford University Press.

Meinong, Alexius. 1972. *On emotional presentation*, trans. M.-L. Schubert Kalsi. Evanston: Northwestern University Press. Original edition: Meinong, Alexius. 1917. Über emotionale Präsentation. Sitzungsberichte der Wiener Akademie der Wissenschaften, phil.-hist. Klasse 183, Abhandlung 2.

Müller, Jean M. 2017. How (not) to think of emotions as evaluative attitudes. *Dialectica* 71 (2): 281–308.

Müller, Jean M. 2011. Emotion, Wahrnehmung, evaluative Erkenntnis. In *Affektive Intentionalität*, ed. Jan Slaby, Achim Stephan, Henrik Walter, and Sven Walter, 110–127. Paderborn: Mentis.

Müller, Jean M. 2019. Dietrich von Hildebrand. In *Routledge handbook of phenomenology of emotions*, ed. Thomas Szanto and Hilge Landweer. London and New York: Routledge. Forthcoming.

Mulligan, Kevin. 2004. Husserl on the "logics" of valuing, values and norms. In *Fenomenologia della ragion pratica*, ed. Beatrice Centi and Gianna Gigliotti, 177–225. Naples: Bibliopolis.

Mulligan, Kevin. 2007. Intentionality, knowledge and formal objects. *Disputatio* 23 (2): 205–228.

Mulligan, Kevin. 2008. Scheler: Die Anatomie des Herzens oder was man alles fühlen kann. In *Klassische Emotionstheorien von Platon bis Wittgenstein*, ed. Hilge Landweer and Ursula Renz, 589–612. Berlin: de Gruyter.

Mulligan, Kevin. 2009. On being struck by value. In *Leben mit Gefühlen*, ed. Barbara Merker, 141–161. Paderborn: Mentis.

Mulligan, Kevin. 2010a. Husserls Herz. In *Husserl und die Philosophie des Geistes*, ed. Manfred Frank and Niels Weidtmann, 209–238. Berlin: Suhrkamp.

Mulligan, Kevin. 2010b. Emotions and values. In *Oxford handbook of the philosophy of emotion*, ed. Peter Goldie, 475–500. Oxford: Oxford University Press.

Pelser, Adam. 2014. Emotion, evaluative perception, and epistemic justification. In *Emotion and value*, ed. Sabine Roeser and Cain Todd, 107–123. Oxford: Oxford University Press.

Poellner, Peter. 2016. Phenomenology and the perceptual model of emotion. *Proceedings of the Aristotelian Society* 116 (3): 261–288.

Reinach, Adolf. 1989. *Sämtliche Werke*, vol. 1. Munich: Philosophia.

Roberts, Robert C. 2003. *Emotions*. Cambridge: Cambridge University Press.

Roberts, Robert C. 2013. *Emotions in the moral life*. Cambridge: Cambridge University Press.

Salice, Alessandro. 2016. The phenomenology of the Göttingen and Munich circles. In *Stanford encyclopedia of philosophy* (Winter edition), ed. Edward Zalta. http://plato.stanford.edu/entries/phenomenology-mg/. Accessed 1 April 2019.

Sartre, Jean-Paul. 1999. *War diaries,* trans. Q. Hoare. London: Verso. Original edition: Sartre, Jean-Paul. 1983. *Les carnets de la drôle de guerre*, ed. Arlette Elkaïm-Sartre. Paris: Gallimard.

Sartre, Jean-Paul. 2002a. Intentionality: A fundamental idea of Husserl's phenomenology. In *The phenomenology reader*, ed. Dermot Moran and Timothy Mooney, 382–384. London and New York: Routledge. Original publication: Sartre, Jean-Paul. 1939. Une idée fondamentale de la phénoménologie de Husserl: l'intentionnalité. *Nouvelle Revue Française* 52: 1939.

Sartre, Jean-Paul. 2002b. *Sketch of a theory of the emotions,* trans. P. Mairet. London and New York: Routledge. Original edition: Sartre, Jean-Paul. 1939. *Esquisse d'une théorie des émotions*. Paris: Hermann.

Sartre, Jean-Paul. 2003. *Being and nothingness,* trans. M. E. Barnes. London and New York: Routledge. Original edition: Sartre, Jean-Paul. 1943. *L'Être et le néant*. Paris: Gallimard.

Sartre, Jean-Paul. 2004. *The transcendence of the ego,* trans. A. Brown. London and New York: Routledge. Original publication: Sartre, Jean-Paul. 1936–1937. La transcendence de l'égo. *Recherches philosophiques* 6: 85–123.

Scheler, Max. 1973. *Formalism in ethics and non-formal ethics of values,* trans. M. S. Frings and R. L. Funk. Evanston, IL: Northwestern University Press. Original edition: Scheler, Max. 1913–1916. *Der Formalismus in der Ethik und die materiale Wertethik*. Halle: Max Niemeyer.

Slaby, Jan. 2008. *Gefühl und Weltbezug*. Paderborn: Mentis.

Tappolet, Christine. 2000. *Émotions et valeurs*. Paris: Presses Universitaires France.

Tappolet, Christine. 2002. Long-term emotions and emotional experiences in the explanation of actions: A critical review of Peter Goldie's *The emotion:*

A philosophical exploration. In *European review of philosophy 5: Emotion and action*, ed. Elisabeth Pacherie, 151–161. Stanford: CSLI Publications.
Tappolet, Christine. 2012. Emotion, perceptions and emotional illusions. In *Perceptual illusions*, ed. Clothilde Calabi, 207–224. Houndsmill: Palgrave Macmillan.
Tappolet, Christine. 2016. *Emotions, values and agency.* Oxford: Oxford University Press.
Teroni, Fabrice. 2007. Emotions and formal objects. *Dialectica* 61 (3): 395–415.
Vendrell Ferran, Íngrid. 2008. *Die Emotionen: Gefühle in der realistischen Phänomenologie.* Berlin: Akademie.
Vendrell Ferran, Íngrid. 2009. Meinongs Philosophie der Gefühle und ihr Einfluss auf die Grazer Schule. In *Meinong Studien* [Meinong studies], vol. 3, ed. Alfred Schramm, 199–239. Graz: Ontos.
Voigtländer, Else. 1910. *Vom Selbstgefühl.* Leipzig: Voigtländer.
von Hildebrand, Dietrich. 1953. *Christian ethics.* New York: McKay.
von Hildebrand, Dietrich. 1969a. *Die Idee der sittlichen Handlung.* Special Edition. Darmstadt: Wissenschaftliche Buchgesellschaft. Original publication: von Hildebrand, Dietrich. 1916. Die Idee der sittlichen Handlung. *Jahrbuch für Philosophie und phänomenologische Forschung* 3: 126–251.
von Hildebrand, Dietrich. 1969b. *Sittlichkeit und ethische Werterkenntnis.* Special Edition. Darmstadt: Wissenschaftliche Buchgesellschaft. Original publication: von Hildebrand, Dietrich. 1922. Sittlichkeit und ethische Werterkenntnis. *Jahrbuch für Philosophie und phänomenologische Forschung* 5: 463–602.
Weberman, David. 1996a. Heidegger and the disclosive character of the emotions. *The Southern Journal of Philosophy* 34 (3): 379–410.
Weberman, David. 1996b. Sartre, emotions, and wallowing. *American Philosophical Quarterly* 33 (4): 393–407.
Whiting, Demian. 2012. Are emotions perceptual experiences of value? *Ratio* 25 (1): 93–107.
Zamuner, Edoardo. 2015. Emotions as psychological reactions. *Mind and Language* 30 (1): 22–43.

4

Emotional Feeling as Position-Taking

Abstract Based on my remarks on feeling towards in the foregoing chapter, I offer the *position-taking view* (PT) as more adequate intentionalist alternative to the axiological receptivity view (AR). On this view, emotional feelings constitute a (dis)favourable position taken towards something in response to its (dis)value. After a brief survey of the early phenomenological pedigree of PT and some appearances of the view and its close cognates in the contemporary literature PT is elaborated and shown to offer a substantive, rather than mere metaphorical account of emotional feeling. More specifically, I argue that the hedonic character of emotional feeling constitutes a felt satisfaction or frustration of specific concerns of the experiencing subject. This makes feeling towards intelligible as a form of (dis)approval and, thereby, as the taking of a (dis)favorable position. Finally PT is contrasted with a recent, apparently similar proposal, according to which emotional feelings are evaluative attitudes (Deonna and Teroni 2012, chapter 7; 2014; 2015).

Keywords Position-taking · Hedonic tone · Feeling towards · Satisfaction/frustration of concerns · (Dis)approval

In the foregoing chapter, I rejected the view that emotional feeling is receptivity to value (AR). The felt inner agitation of an emotion does not disclose the corresponding formal object. The phenomenology of emotional feelings and the ways in which we ordinarily ascribe and make sense of them show AR to be in sharp tension with the manifest image of emotion, which supports a radically different view. According to this view, the emotional feeling is *feeling towards*, a specific type of response to value.

In this chapter, I argue that the view of emotional feeling that I opposed to AR does not merely show it to be mistaken. Rather, the recognition of emotional feeling as feeling towards at the same time makes available a different intentionalist account. According to this account, emotional feeling is a specific type of *position-taking* rather than receptivity or 'cognizance-taking': to emotionally feel towards an object is to adopt a (dis)favourable position towards it in response to value. I initially offer a basic exposition of the position-taking view (PT), which parallels a number of extant proposals in the early realist phenomenologist and contemporary literature (Sect. 1). In the main part of this chapter, I offer a more detailed explication of PT on the basis of a more thorough account of the hedonic tone of emotional feeling (Sect. 2). I there elaborate in detail the proposal that emotional feeling is a specific form of position-taking, which bears an intimate connection to our cares and concerns. I finally contrast PT with a recent proposal that purports to be a close cognate (Sect. 3).

1   The Idea

In contrasting emotional and perceptual experience from the perspective of the experiencing subject, I claimed that emotion involves a felt inner agitation which is directed or aimed at something. In this context, I also hinted at a somewhat richer account which is suggested by von Hildebrand's comparison between emotions and speech acts: in emotional feeling we 'speak' rather than 'listen' to the world. I proposed that this metaphor invites thinking of emotional feelings as ways of taking a position on the world. Insofar in joy or pride we feel good about something, we take a *favourable position* towards it. Corresponding characterizations can be given of negative and hedonically mixed emotional feelings. In indignation, one feels bother or discomfort towards something. Insofar as one's discomfort is aimed at a certain event or state of affairs, one takes a *disfavourable position* towards it. In feeling nostalgic one's position is favourable, albeit in a qualified sense. While nostalgia is pleasant, the feeling aimed at one's past also involves some pain or discomfort. Thus, in this case one's position on the world is ambivalent.

These considerations intuitively suggest that emotional feeling plays a specific kind of psychological role that contrasts with the role accorded to it by AR. Rather than apprehending or 'taking cognizance' of aspects of its circumstances, the felt agitation of emotion is a way of taking a stand or position on such aspects. My use of the term "position-taking" in this context goes back to the German early realist phenomenological tradition that I have been referring to in criticizing AR.[1] The first prominent appearance of this term, as applied to emotion, can be found in von Hildebrand (1969 [1916], 11):

> If we consider joy about something, enthusiasm, longing, love for something, all these experiences reveal a common character. Despite their qualitative differences they constitute *position-takings* of my self towards the world of objects. The moment of joy or the moment of enthusiasm are contents (*Gehalte*), which are embedded into the experience on the side of the *subject*, and which are *directed towards* (*gelten*) a content (*Inhalt*) before me. (own transl.)

What von Hildebrand calls the "moment" or "content" ("*Gehalt*") of an emotion can be seen to correspond to the specific intentional mode (or, in Husserl's language, 'act quality') of that emotion (e.g. joy, enthusiasm).[2] It is also plausibly understood as the specific way one feels in having that emotion. Von Hildebrand describes the content of a position-taking (in part) as what one is 'filled with' in taking a stand and also refers to it as a 'content in the soul' (cf. e.g. 1953, 177f.). What we are filled with in having an emotion is a particular feeling—a feeling in the soul or sensitive mind. Moreover, he uses the term to refer to the same aspect of position-

---

[1]On the history of the notion of position-taking cf. Mulligan (2013). On the history of the view that emotions are position-takings cf. Mulligan (2017, 229ff.) and Müller (2019, section 1).

[2]On von Hildebrand's account of emotion as position-taking cf. also Müller (2019, section 1).

takings he occasionally metaphorically describes as a positive or negative 'inner word' which is imparted to their object (cf. esp. 1953, chapter 18). In line with my earlier remarks on von Hildebrand's speech act metaphor, it makes sense to think of an 'inner word' as imparted to the world in position-taking insofar as one has a directed hedonic feeling: one takes a (dis)favourable stand on the world in feeling good or bad towards it.[3] In this passage, von Hildebrand does not explicitly refer to the character of emotional feelings as responses to value, but he highlights this aspect in various other places throughout this and later works (e.g. (1969 [1916], 37ff.; 1953, chapter 18).

A look at the more recent literature suggests that the alternative account of the significance of emotional feeling I have sketched, or a very close cognate, is espoused also by certain contemporary authors.[4] Consider the following passage from Mulligan (2010a, 234), who himself draws on the early realist phenomenological tradition.

> It is hard to deny that emotions are reactions, resp. have the character of responses. […] Indeed, the fact that so many emotions are positive or negative and thus have a "valence" just means that these emotions are reactions, position-takings for or against something. (own transl.)

To be fair, Mulligan's proposal allows for multiple readings depending on how the notion of valence is interpreted in this context.[5] If Mulligan's use of the term "valence" is interpreted as referring to the hedonic tone of occurrent emotion, he can be understood as claiming that emotions are position-takings for or against something *insofar as they are (un)pleasant*. I am inclined to adopt this reading in line of what Mulligan says in other places (cf. e.g. Mulligan and Scherer 2012, 320).[6] Sometimes, Mulligan

---

[3]Von Hildebrand himself does not use the terms "favour" and "disfavour". But he highlights the affirmative character of the positions taken in positive emotions, such as joy and love. Cf. (1953, 220).

[4]In what follows, I restrict myself to authors that directly endorse PT or views that are very close cognates. I refer to further, similar proposals in the later sections of this chapter.

[5]A very helpful critical survey is given by Colombetti (2005).

[6]That said, taking inspiration from Scheler (1973 [1913–1916]), Mulligan seems to understand (un)pleasantness as an axiological property instead of a way of feeling. The view is discussed in some more detail (though not explicitly endorsed) in Mulligan (2010b, 492ff.). In this respect, the

also uses the terms "pro attitude" and "con attitude" (e.g. 2004, 217; 2007, 210) and, in accordance with my account above, "favour" and "disfavour" (2007, 209, 222). While in this passage, Mulligan does not explicitly refer to position-taking that is responsive to *value*, much of what he says elsewhere clearly suggests that he conceives of it in this way (cf. e.g. 2007, 224, 226; 2010b, 485).

In a similar vein, though taking his lead from research in social psychology, Gaus (1990, 68f.) proposes that the felt aspect of an emotion is a liking or disliking, where the relevant sense of "(dis)liking" is supposed to be akin to "having a (dis)favourable attitude towards". Gaus does not commit to the view that emotional feelings are (dis)pleasures, though he does not seem entirely unsympathetic to it either (cf. ibid., 68f.). Moreover, Gaus recognizes a link between emotional feeling and value that seems to come close to the responsive connection I have highlighted in that he takes it that emotional feelings are, at least in many cases, justified and triggered by evaluative beliefs (ibid., chapter 6 and 8.2). That said, Gaus does not explicitly recognize the felt aspect of an emotion as directed at a certain object *in response to* (apparent) axiological features of it. To say that an emotional feeling is caused and justified by an axiological belief is not to say that it responds to an (apparent) exemplification of value, i.e. to the object of a state of awareness (as) of value.[7] Note, also, that Gaus at the same time shows some sympathy for AR (cf. ibid., 159).

The idea that an emotion is a positive or negative position-taking in virtue of having hedonic valence is espoused also by Vendrell Ferran (2008, chapter 6). Like Mulligan, Vendrell Ferran takes her inspiration from the early phenomenological tradition. Unlike Mulligan, however, Vendrell Ferran restricts this conception to a subset of emotions. She explicitly argues that certain emotions—those she calls "personality emotions"—are

---

conception he articulates in the above passage may seem to differ from the view I have sketched. I take Mulligan's position to be a very close cognate to PT as I have introduced the view, though.

[7] Remember that reasons for which one is in a given intentional state are not mere causes of this state, but reasons *for which* one is in that state. Cf. Sect. 3 in Chapter 3. Perhaps the condition that the respective evaluative belief both causes *and justifies* the feeling is supposed to make it intelligible as a reason for which one has it. But this conception does not make sense of the idea that emotional feeling is a response to an (apparent) exemplification of value as opposed to a response to an evaluative belief. However, this is intuitively important: we have emotional feelings towards a given object in light of (apparent) axiological aspects of it, not in light of our own mental states.

positive or negative position-takings regardless of their (dis)pleasurable dimension. On her view, love, hatred, admiration and existential envy, are positive or negative position-takings independently of having hedonic tone. Indeed, Vendrell Ferran (2008, 170) denies that some of these emotions have a stable hedonic tone to begin with and supposes that they are positive position-takings even when they are unpleasant (pleasant).[8] As noted in Sect. 3 in Chapter 3, she also denies that these are responses to value.

We find a further cognate view in Greenspan (1980). Greenspan speaks of a specific class of emotions as pro or con attitudes and explicitly says that these "seem to involve taking 'positions,' of sorts, on their object [...]" (ibid., 229). Moreover, these emotions are conceived as (dis)pleasures. However, in characterizing (dis)pleasure as an attitude, she supposes that it is not a feeling. Also, Greenspan remains silent on the connection between emotion and value.

In a similar vein, in offering a specific reconstruction of Scheler's and Sartre's views on emotion, Poellner (2016) discusses a specific subset of emotions—emotions that are intelligible or make sense to their subject—of which he gives a cognate characterization. These (or at least some of them) "typically include a valenced (positive or negative) affective component, a felt approval or disapproval" (ibid., 264). This suggests that they are conceived as position-takings since, intuitively, in approving or disapproving of something one takes a positive or negative stand on it. Poellner alternatively also speaks, in the positive case, of a "felt favouring" (ibid., 266). He does not explicitly claim that this component is a case of (dis)pleasure, but seems to think of it as a kind of felt 'attraction' or 'repulsion' (ibid., 266). Also, Poellner ultimately thinks of this felt aspect as registering value and denies that it is a response to previously registered values. In line with a specific interpretation of Scheler's and Sartre's view on value, felt (dis)approval is thought to constitute an "uptake" of a value's demand to be or remain actual. Since in characterizing this experience,

---

[8] The issue of the stability of hedonic tone was discussed in Sect. 2 in Chapter 2, where I defend the view that emotions have a stable hedonic core against what I take to be the most salient counter-examples. Vendrell Ferran's view is supported in part also by considerations on the intensity of emotion. As she proposes (2008, 171), love and admiration can be intense without this intensity being reflected in an equally intense hedonic tone.

he also refers to Sartre's claim that in some emotions values are 'given' or presented (2003 [1943], 62), I take him to be committed to a qualified version of AR.[9]

Since some of the authors I have here mentioned conceive of (at least some) emotions as position-takings independently of having hedonic tone, there is perhaps a question as to whether hedonic tone is generally apt to qualify emotions as position-takings. As far as I can see, as long as we can think of each emotion as having a stable hedonic core and as directed, the intuition that emotions are position-takings insofar as they are hedonic is a fairly strong one. (This point should moreover be corroborated by how I elaborate the view in what follows.) Relatedly, I think that, intuitively, the dimensions of 'attraction' and 'repulsion' Poellner refers to are less readily intelligible as cases of (dis)favouring or (dis)approval than directed (dis)pleasure. I might add that I also disagree with Vendrell Ferran that the class of emotions she has in mind are plausibly thought of as position-takings independently of hedonic tone. In contrast to her, I do not think that any emotions lack a stable dimension of (dis)pleasure or that their character as a positive or negative position-taking can come apart from their hedonic tone. Although I agree that, for example, in certain cases the hedonic dimension of a positive position-taking like love can be less salient (as e.g. in the case of unrequited erotic love), what is purportedly a different hedonic tone (unpleasantness) in such cases is not an aspect of the emotion proper (cf. Sect. 2.1 in Chapter 2). Thus, in this type of case, the hedonic valence of the emotion and its character as a positive position-taking coincide after all.[10]

---

[9]The idea that emotions have polarity is central also to Zamuner's (2015) view that emotions are psychological reactions. Zamuner takes his lead from Mulligan, though his notion of a reaction is broader than Mulligan's and covers also simple bodily reactions rather than only responses. Cf. Sect. 3 in Chapter 3, n. 21. As noted earlier (Sect. 1.2 in Chapter 2, n. 27), Zamuner explicates the polarity of emotion in terms of a distinction between emotions involving approach and emotions involving avoidance. Importantly, his explication deviates from the standard notion of valence and carries no commitment to the distinction between positive or negative emotions. Also, as previously noted, it is not concerned directly with emotional feeling, though it, plausibly, does have implications for a conception of the phenomenal aspect of some emotions. Cf. (ibid., 30). It is worth stressing also that Zamuner does not recognize emotions as responses to value. Cf. Sect. 3 in Chapter 3, n. 29.

A further, apparently closely related proposal – the 'attitudinal view' proposed by Deonna and Teroni (2012, chapter 7; 2014, 2015)—is discussed in Sect. 3.

[10]To be fair, more would need to be said here also on Vendrell Ferran's considerations regarding intensity. I take it that her view that intensity of emotion and intensity of hedonic tone need not

I should note, moreover, that, in contrast to some of the authors I have mentioned, I will avoid using the term "pro/con attitude" and stick to "(dis)favourable position-taking" and "(dis)approval" since the first term has acquired a technical use in the philosophy of mind that is misplaced in this context. Philosophers of mind commonly speak of "pro/con attitudes" in order to refer to the class of intentional phenomena that have *world-to-mind* direction of fit. For an intentional phenomenon to have world-to-mind direction of fit is for it to aim at changing the world so as for it to conform to its intentional content (where this change is considered sufficient for its satisfaction). In this respect, it contrasts with mental phenomena with *mind-to-world* direction of fit, which put forward their intentional content as correct, that is, aim at fitting the world as it is and are satisfied when they succeed in doing so (cf. Searle 1983). Thus, desire is usually taken to be the paradigm example of a mental state with world-to-mind direction of fit, whilst belief is the paradigm example of state with mind-to-world direction of fit. Note that it seems generally misleading to refer to emotions or their felt aspects as aiming to change the world in such a way as to satisfy them. Thus, it makes no sense to think that your joy or the way you feel towards the scene you are watching aims to change the world in a way that would conform to its intentional content and thereby satisfy it (cf. also Deonna and Teroni 2012, 10f.; 2014, 2015). Perhaps certain future-directed emotions constitute exceptions in this respect. Being/feeling hopeful that a certain state of affairs obtains might be thought to involve an affirmation of that state of affairs in a sense that aims at realizing this state of affairs. However, in the majority of cases, the attribution of world-to-mind direction to fit to emotions or their felt aspects makes no sense. Indeed, in many cases emotions have no intentional content that would make them amenable to assessments in terms of direction of fit to begin with. In many cases they take objects that are not propositionally structured (e.g. dogs in the case of fear, people or their qualities in the case of admiration etc.). Our common ways of ascribing them and their phenomenology seem to testify to this (cf. Sect. 2

---

coincide is plausible only when "intensity" is not read as qualifying the felt aspect of emotion. The topic of emotional intensity raises a number of issues, though, which I here will not be able to do justice to.

in Chapter 3).[11] In contrast to the technical use of "pro/con attitude", the use of "(dis)favourable position-taking" and "(dis)approval" does not imply that the phenomenon to which the term is applied has any direction of fit.[12]

So far, my exposition of PT has been relatively superficial. While there is arguably something intuitive to this proposal, one might wonder about the precise sense in which one can be said to take a particular position towards something in having an emotional feeling. Perhaps one might even wonder whether the view can ultimately offer more than a metaphor. As PT has been expounded so far, it may seem to gain its pre-theoretically plausibility largely from figurative considerations such as von Hildebrand's characterization of emotional feeling as a type of speech act. However, if PT is to be a fully satisfactory intentionalist alternative to AR, we should be able to give a substantive, rather than metaphorical, account of the notion of an emotional position-taking. In the main part of this chapter, I show that this is possible and explain in which respect precisely the notion of a position-taking has literal application to emotional feeling.

2 Substantiating the Notion of Emotional Position-Taking

There are multiple ways to further elaborate PT. As I noted in the Introduction, the view that emotions are evaluative judgments (e.g. Nussbaum 2001) can be understood as recognizing emotions as position-takings. In the early phenomenological literature, judgment and belief are conceived as directed towards propositional contents (or the states of affairs characterized by them) and count as intellectual position-takings towards these contents (states of affairs). On this view, in judging or believing that p one takes a positive position towards p in response to its apparent truth (obtaining). This position differs from the position one adopts in disbe-

---

[11] This criticism touches on an issue raised by Deonna and Teroni (2012, chapter 7; 2014, 2015). Cf. also Müller (2017). I return to Deonna and Teroni's view of emotion in Sect. 3.

[12] In this context, I prefer "position-taking" also to "stance", since the latter is also sometimes used to refer to a more general outlook, perspective or explanatory strategy. Cf. e.g. Dennett's (1987) use of the terms "intentional stance", "functional stance" etc.

lieving that *p*, which is a negative position towards that proposition (state of affairs) in response to its apparent falsity (lack of obtaining of the corresponding state of affairs). Perhaps it will also seem that this characterization is readily intelligible as literal, rather than metaphorical. Intuitively, it can seem that judging is clearly a paradigm of position-taking. To arrive at a judgment about whether *p* is, effectively, to make a verdict about the matter, which one might suppose is a bona fide case of taking a stand. If so, then it seems that the view that emotions are evaluative judgments can be understood as giving a substantive account of them as position-takings. What is more, in the case of Nussbaum (2001), the view seems in fact to be concerned predominantly with emotional feeling: it is in being emotionally affected that one judgementally assents to a certain evaluative content. For example, the following passage suggests that, for her, to be properly affected by something (in this case a loss) is a cognitive act of recognizing an evaluative content (which, to Nussbaum, is the same as an act of judging an evaluative content). Here, the notion of upheaval partly characterizes this affective aspect:

> [...] the real, full recognition of that terrible event [...] *is* the upheaval. It is [...] like putting a nail into your stomach. [...] If I go up to embrace the death image [a value-laden image of her mother as dead, JMM], if I take it into myself as the way things are, it is at that very moment, in that cognitive act itself, that I am putting the world's nail into my own insides. That is not preparation for upheaval, that is upheaval itself. (2001, 45)

Accordingly, one way in which one might think of substantiating PT is in terms of a judgmentalist picture of emotional feeling: emotional feelings are position-takings insofar as they are ways of intellectually assenting to an evaluative content (state of affairs) in response to the real or mere apparent truth (obtaining) of that content (state of affairs). On this picture, emotions are responses to apparent exemplifications of their formal object insofar as they are responsive to the apparent truth (obtaining) of evaluative propositions (states of affairs) featuring their formal object.[13]

I believe there are various issues with this proposal. Although it is perhaps compelling to suppose that judgment is a paradigm of position-taking, the view faces well-known difficulties insofar as it assimilates emotions to intellectual phenomena. The most familiar objection is that judging a specific evaluative content is simply not sufficient for the corresponding emotion.[14] Thus, it is perfectly possible to judge that some object or event is dangerous without being afraid. Nussbaum tries to address this worry by emphasizing that the evaluative content of the relevant judgments is intimately connected with one's cares and concerns or, as she puts it, with aspects of one's own well-being (2001, chapter 1). In line with my proposed account of formal objects, on her view, to feel afraid is to judge a content which represents the object of fear as important insofar as it negatively bears on a specific concern. Judging this type of content is supposed to be impossible without being emotionally affected. However, this is doubtful: we can imagine someone in a state of anhedonia or depression who judges that some object or event poses a threat to something she is attached to and is thus incongruent with that attachment without her feeling afraid.[15] Note, moreover, that judgmentalism also seems to misrepresent the intentionality of emotion. Judgments are directed at propositions or propositionally structured entities (states of affairs). Judgmentalism thus takes emotions to have propositionally structured targets. Yet emotions and their felt aspects seem often not to be directed towards propositionally structured entities. If this is correct it is also false to think of them as responsive to truth (obtaining). Emotions are responsive to aspects of their target. Clearly, where the target is non-

---

[13] In line with the disjunctive picture sketched in Sect. 3 in Chapter 3, the emotion can be thought of as a response to the truth of a proposition (the obtaining of a state of affairs) when the appearance is a case of awareness.

[14] This objection is widely raised against judgmentalism about emotion. Cf. e.g. Deonna and Teroni (2012, chapter 5) for a thorough discussion.

[15] Nussbaum (2001, 41) insists that in such cases one does not actually or properly judge the proposition in question. This strikes me as dogmatic. What is missing in such cases seems not to be intellectual.

propositional, it is not something that can be true or false (obtain or fail to obtain[16]).[17]

The account I offer in what follows opts for a different route and thus avoids the difficulties faced by judgmentalism. As far as I can see, there is a way to make sense of the notion of emotional position-taking which gets by without assimilating emotional feelings to intellectual phenomena. Rather, it recognizes them as position-takings in their own right.

As expounded above, PT gains some of its intuitive appeal from the observation that emotional feeling is both hedonic and directed. If emotional feelings possess both hedonic tone and directedness, this makes it compelling to suppose that they in some sense positively or negatively aim at particular objects. And this characterization in turn is evocative of the view that they constitute a positive or negative stand or position toward those objects. In order to show that this view is apt and make it intelligible as a substantive rather than metaphorical account, we must provide some further elucidation of the hedonic character of emotional feeling. As I will show in what follows, suitably explicated, the notion of hedonic tone shows emotions to be position-takings inasmuch as it makes them intelligible as specific forms of approval or disapproval. As I said above in connection with Poellner's (2016) view, it seems intuitive to suppose that in (dis)approving of something one takes a positive (negative) position toward it. Moreover, we can make more explicit what is involved in (dis)approval in a way that is sensitive to this intuition. While Poellner (2016) does not further explicate the notion of (dis)approval in this respect, it seems to me that the following is a rather natural account that captures this intuition: to (dis)approve of something is to *find it (dis)agreeable*, that

---

[16] Non-propositionally structured targets (such as material objects and property-instances) may be actual or not. But only states of affairs can obtain or fail to obtain.

[17] There are further issues with judgmentalism. Cf. e.g. Teroni (2007), Deonna and Teroni (2012, chapter 5). Cf. also von Hildebrand (1953, chapter 18) for an interesting account of the differences between intellectual and affective position-takings.

The first of the above raised problems for judgmentalism does not affect a related proposal, according to which emotional feelings constitute a distinctive, non-intellectual form of assent. Cf. Helm (2001, 45f., 64ff.) and Slaby (2008, 242f.). However, inasmuch as this proposal is to be intelligible as invoking a genuine notion of assent it must also (erroneously) conceive of emotions as directed at propositionally structured entities. Moreover, Helm and Slaby understand emotional feeling to simultaneously apprehend value. Accordingly, they do not get into proper focus the idea that, as a response to value, affect occurs *on the basis of* grasp of value.

is, concordant (discordant) with oneself or one's evaluative outlook. To give a substantive account of the idea of emotional position-taking, I will thus argue that the hedonic dimension of emotion is precisely a form of concordance (discordance) with oneself, which is directed towards something. The way in which I substantiate PT in what follows has thus far not been proposed by any of the adherents of PT or cognate views I have listed above, though I think it is reasonably congenial to the core idea of the view whilst elucidating what is pre-theoretically plausible about it.

2.1   The Personal Dimension of Hedonic Tone

In Sect. 1 in Chapter 2, I claimed that the felt agitation of emotion possesses a personal dimension: *we*—as subjects with certain cares and concerns—are affected in particular way. To feel afraid is to be affected as someone who *is attached to* something (e.g. one's bodily, mental or social integrity), to feel angry is to be touched as someone who *upholds* and thus *cares about* certain norms or standards. More generally, in occurrent emotion, we are always affected as someone who is to a certain extent invested into something. In defending the claim that emotional feeling is a form of psychic (dis)comfort in Sect. 1.2 in Chapter 2, I precisified this idea to a certain extent by noting that, in having an emotion, we feel (un)comfortable inasmuch as something in one way or another positively or negatively resonates with our cares and concerns. Thus, in fear, we feel uncomfortable inasmuch something palpably frustrates our attachment to something. In anger, we feel bothered or uncomfortable inasmuch as something contravenes our concern to be treated in a specific, respectful or dignified way. Similarly, the pleasantness of one's joy after having completed a good day's work seems intimately linked to one's desire to meet one's goals for the day: we feel good insofar as this desire is palpably satisfied.

Considerations on these lines motivate an account of emotional (dis)pleasure defended by Roberts (2003). According to Roberts, emotional (dis)pleasure consists in the "perceived satisfaction or frustration of a concern by a situation" (ibid., 157).[18] While I take this proposal to be by and large correct, there are two respects in which this view requires qualification. I address these in turn.

First, it is important to clarify the idea of the satisfaction or frustration of a concern. In giving an account of emotional (dis)pleasure, the satisfaction or frustration of concerns must be sharply distinguished from the positive or negative value to which the emotion is responsive. This is important since, as I proposed in Sect. 2.2 in Chapter 2 and Sect. 5 in Chapter 3, this value can be thought of as constituted (at least in part) by the positive or negative significance or relevance which something has relative to particular concerns. And it can seem that the positive or negative relevance of something for a concern coincides with its satisfaction or frustration, respectively.[19]

However, this impression is mistaken. To think of something as positively or negatively relevant to a concern is not to think of it as positively or negatively resonating with (satisfying or frustrating) that concern. The former is to recognize it as objectively (in)congruent with this concern. In contrast, in the latter case we refer to an actual psychological occurrence in which this concern is favourably or adversely impinged upon in a specific way. This distinction is worth stressing since satisfaction and frustration are often equated with the objective (in)congruence of things with concerns. At least in the case of desires, it is usually supposed that they are satisfied insofar as they bring about changes which make the world congruent with (render true) their intentional content. My account of satisfaction and frustration crucially differs from a mere semantic understanding of these notions in conceiving of satisfaction and frustration as actual psy-

---

[18] The same idea is found in Schroeder (2007). A cognate view is held by Wollheim (1999). In this connection, cf. also Düringer (2014, chapter 6) on positive emotions. These authors focus on the satisfaction or frustration specifically of desires. As I understand concerns, they include also interests, aversions, needs, preferences, attachments and valuings. Deonna and Teroni (2012, 33ff.) raise several objections to views that identify emotions with representations of the satisfaction (frustration) of desires. Though I here lack the space to fully address these, it seems to me that they are less threatening to a view on which hedonic tone consists in the felt satisfaction (frustration) of concerns more generally, as elaborated below. At least the view I shall elaborate is not committed to an objectionable meta-representational analysis of emotions or emotional feelings. Cf. n. 22. Given a suitably liberal notion of concern, it neither seems to me to distort the variety and richness of emotional experience.

[19] Roberts (2003) is not always sufficiently clear about the difference between these.

chological occurrences.[20] On this account, the objective (in)congruence of something with a concern is neither necessary nor sufficient for its satisfaction (frustration). It is not necessary since the satisfaction (frustration) of concerns may be a response to mere apparent (in)congruence with them: in the relevant, psychological sense the satisfaction of my concern to meet my goals for the day requires only that the world *seems* congruent with it. Concern (in)congruence is not sufficient for concern satisfaction (frustration) either since the fact of something's being (in)congruent with a concern does not entail that one registers the (in)congruence and responds accordingly.

A second qualification concerns the term "perceived" in this context. The claim that emotional (dis)pleasure consists in the perceived satisfaction (frustration) of concerns invites misconceptions. In particular, it can seem to come dangerously close to an epistemic conception of emotional feeling: Does it not amount to the claim that emotional feelings present or register the satisfaction or frustration of concerns? And have I not argued that they are directed in a sense that is incompatible with them being presentations or ways of registering something? We can disperse this worry if we instead characterize hedonic tone as the *felt* satisfaction (frustration) of a concern and understand "feel the satisfaction (frustration) of a concern" adverbially, that is, as ascribing a *way of feeling* rather than awareness of concern satisfaction (frustration). We thereby take account of the fact that emotional (dis)pleasure is canonically ascribed by the adverbial construction "feel good (bad)". Note that this construction refers to a way of feeling, rather than an awareness of something. In this respect, it differs from the transitive construction "feel the goodness (badness) of *x*". On the analysis I propose, ascriptions of emotional (dis)pleasure by the transitive construction "feel the satisfaction (frustration) of a concern" ascribe what is also ascribed by "feel good (bad)". That is, they refer to concern satisfaction (frustration) understood as a *way of feeling*.[21] This proposal

---

[20] In this respect, this account is similar to Wollheim's (1999, 8ff.) psychologized account of desire satisfaction (frustration). While in agreement with the core of Wollheim's view, there are some respects in which my account is different. I here lack the space to discuss these, but hope to do so in the context of a more thorough discussion of Wollheim's overall theory of emotion in future work.

[21] Accordingly, the terms "good" and "bad" do not refer to axiological properties in this context or to what I call (in)congruence with concerns. As for the type of psychological occurrence that they

is compatible with the claim that emotional feeling is not a case of registering or apprehending something, but a feeling towards something: the way we feel in having an emotion is directed towards a particular object or event.[22]

We can motivate this analysis by noting that adverbial analyses of transitive "feel" constructions make good sense in a closely related context. Consider the transitive constructions "feel satisfaction" and "feel frustration". To say of someone that she feels satisfaction (frustration) is tantamount to saying that she feels satisfied (frustrated). We thereby ascribe a certain *way of feeling* rather than awareness of an emotion.[23] This way of feeling can be characterized as positive (negative): it is a case of feeling good (bad). Thus, ascriptions of this form are analysable in adverbial terms, where the ascribed way of feeling is picked out also by "feel good (bad)". I propose to similarly analyse "feel the satisfaction (frustration) of a concern". Now, one cannot simply analyse this locution as being synonymous with "feel frustrated (satisfied)" at pains of assimilating all emotional (dis)pleasure to the way of feeling characteristic of the specific emotions of satisfaction and frustration. But there is a related analysis on which this locution picks out a corresponding, qualified way of feeling: feeling satisfied or frustrated *as the subject of specific concerns*. Thus, I understand talk of feeling the satisfaction (frustration) of a particular concern as talk of feeling satisfied (frustrated) as a subject of that concern, where this way of feeling is also what answers to "feel good (bad)", as used to refer to emotional (dis)pleasure more generally. I take this adverbial analysis to make good sense given the plausibility of the adverbial analysis of "feel satisfaction (frustration)". In this context, I correspondingly understand "good" ("bad") as referring to ways one feels (frustrated/satisfied) qua subject of certain concerns. This adverbial analysis of "feel the satisfaction (frustration) of a concern" accommodates for the intimate connection between

---

pick out (satisfaction or frustration of a concern), I am inclined to think that it is intrinsically felt, that is, a way of feeling. However, there is no need to insist on this as long as emotional hedonic tone is identified explicitly with the *felt* satisfaction (frustration) of a concern.

[22]This analysis also avoids conceiving emotions or their felt aspects as meta-representations of concerns and thus one of Deonna and Teroni's (2012, 35) worries with the identification of emotions with representations of desire satisfaction (frustration).

[23]I here depart from the analysis of emotional feeling Roberts gives in (2003, chapter 4, section 3).

emotional feeling and the satisfaction or frustration of cares and concerns without compromising their character as feelings towards.

Despite what one might initially suppose, this analysis accommodates also the hedonic tone of the specific emotions satisfaction and frustration. Although the way we ordinarily ascribe these emotions seems to imply that it is the person as such rather than particular concerns of hers that is satisfied (frustrated), we can account for the relevant intuitive distinction by supposing that the concerns in these cases have a special standing. When I report not simply joy but satisfaction after having completed a good day's work, the comfort of my emotion is still tied specifically to the fate of my desire to meet my goals for the day. In this case, however, the desire has a particular standing in being central to my evaluative perspective or at least presently takes a prominent place within my personal investments. It is for this reason that we here commonly speak of satisfaction *simpliciter*.[24]

In light of this account of emotional (dis)pleasure, it is now but a small step towards completing my elaboration of PT. In the next sub-section, I explain how this account makes sense of emotions as forms of (dis)approval.

2.2 Hedonic Tone as Position-Taking

The proposed view of hedonic tone does not only make explicit the personal dimension of emotional feeling. It also renders emotional feelings intelligible as ways of finding the world (dis)agreeable. To see this, it is crucial to recognize the satisfaction (frustration) of concerns as a way in which the world is concordant (discordant) with our evaluative outlook. The relevant notion of concordance (discordance) is a specifically expe-

---

[24] As Roberts (2003, 216f.) argues, frustration involves seeing a desire as opposed by a significant obstacle. I take it that this is what the emotion is typically responsive to, though unlike Roberts I do not take this construal to be constitutive of the emotion and moreover doubt that the relevant concern has to be a desire. On the view I propose, the felt aspect of this emotion is identical with the felt frustration of the relevant concern in the sense explicated above. On this picture, we can still recognize feeling frustration as different from the displeasure characteristic of other negative emotions if we take it that the relevant concern enjoys a certain prominence within one's wider set of cares and that this affects how it feels for it to be frustrated.

riential notion. It is paradigmatically expressed in ordinary discourse in first person reports of the following form:

X (the scene/the weather/her new haircut…) (dis)agrees with me

Such statements usually report that something is concordant (discordant) with oneself in a particular sense: it is (not) to one's taste or liking. At the same time, they are reports of (dis)pleasure: what (dis)agrees with one *ipso facto* (dis)pleases one. This notion of concordance (discordance) with oneself makes emotions intelligible as forms of (dis)approval once we appreciate that it covers a rather broad range of (dis)pleasures. Thus, while concordance (discordance) with one's taste or liking can be understood in a somewhat restrictive sense, as referring to a specific set of (broadly) aesthetic cares, there is also a corresponding notion which refers to our personal investments more generally. The pleasantness of one's joy after having completed a good day's work is a case of the world being in agreement with oneself as someone desiring to meet their goals for the day; the bother of indignation is a case of disagreement with oneself as someone with certain normative concerns or values. The proposed account of hedonic tone invokes a broader notion of (dis)agreement with one's concerns on these lines. Emotional (dis)pleasure is concordance (discordance) with one's concerns in the form of their satisfaction (frustration): one feels satisfied ('agreed with') or frustrated ('disagreed with') as a subject of specific concerns.

On the basis of this notion of (dis)agreement we can now make sense of emotional feelings as forms of (dis)approval. To do so, it is important to bear in mind that emotional feelings are directed in the specific sense exposed in the foregoing chapter. Rather than just being ways of feeling satisfied or frustrated as someone with specific concerns, they are ways of feeling satisfied or frustrated as someone with specific concerns *towards* something. How we feel is directed at an object or event qua (dis)valuable. Insofar as the (dis)comfort of emotion is directed (dis)agreement, it becomes intelligible as a way of finding something (dis)agreeable. That is, for one to feel good or bad towards something in having an emotion is for one to find it concordant or discordant with oneself as a subject with specific cares. It is because one's way of feeling (agreed with/disagreed with) is directed towards (aimed at) something that we can characterize it as a case of *finding that thing* concordant or discordant with oneself and thus as a form of (dis)approval. In line with my remarks on the responsive character of emotional feeling, we can add that this (dis)agreement is a response to a particular value. More specifically, given the understanding of formal objects I have introduced, emotional feelings can be conceived as ways of finding something (dis)agreeable relative to particular concerns, which respond to its apparent relevance with respect to those concerns.

These remarks complete my elaboration of PT and show how the view can be plausibly explicated so as to give a substantive account of emotional feeling as position-taking in the sense of (dis)approval. Having spelled out PT in this way and indicated in which precise sense we can think of emotional feeling as position-taking, I would finally like to contrast the view with a further cognate proposal. In Sect. 1 of this chapter, I have already referred to some historical and contemporary authors who endorse PT or some close cognate view, though they do not explicitly develop the view along the lines proposed here. In the final section, I would like to briefly compare PT with Deonna and Teroni's (2012, chapter 7; 2014, 2015) recent account of emotions as evaluative attitudes. On the face of it, this view comes very close to PT as well. Yet, as I argue below, this impression is somewhat misleading.[25]

3 Emotional Feeling as Position-Taking and as Evaluative Attitude

Deonna and Teroni's account is put forward as a view of emotion, but is ultimately developed in terms of their felt aspect. Their core idea is a specific analogy between emotions and other intentional phenomena with formal objects. As they note, in the case of phenomena with formal objects, it is generally because of the intentional mode (in Searle's (1983)

---

[25] Zamuner's (2015) view of emotions as psychological reactions would seem to make for a further interesting comparison. However, Zamuner is not concerned specifically with emotional feeling. Also, given the attention Deonna and Teroni's attitudinal view has recently attracted, it seems more appropriate to devote the rest of this chapter to the latter. For some further (dis)similarities with Zamuner's view cf. Sect. 3 in Chapter 3, n. 21 and n. 29 as well as Sect. 1 in this chapter, n. 9.

terminology, corresponding to Husserl's 'act quality'), not because of the intentional content, of the respective phenomenon that its conditions of fittingness involve the corresponding formal object. As they propose, it is because S adopts the intentional mode of fear towards x that her mental state is fitting if and only if x is dangerous. Fear is the mode of *taking-as-dangerous* an intentional content. In this respect, emotions seem to be on a par with beliefs: it is because S adopts the intentional mode of belief towards the proposition that p that her mental state is fitting if and only if p is true. Belief is the mode of *taking-as-true* an intentional (propositional) content. As Deonna and Teroni go on to develop their view, it is specifically the felt aspect of emotion which is constitutive of the intentional modes of emotions and thereby accounts for the fact that their mode contributes the respective formal object to their conditions of fittingness.

I have assessed this proposal and developed my own version of the view that emotions are evaluative modes elsewhere (cf. Müller 2017). In contrasting Deonna and Teroni's account with the account defended in this chapter, I should stress that their core notion of an attitude is Searle's notion of intentional mode rather than that of position-taking. Importantly, this is a technical notion that applies to all intentional phenomena, including perception and any other form of apprehension. To be fair, Deonna and Teroni's view does have some echoes with PT. For example, in explicating their view they also sometimes speak of emotions as stances or postures we adopt towards the world (e.g. 2012, 79, 81; 2015, 302) and they seem to sympathize with authors whom they take to hold the view that emotions are position-takings.[26] Relatedly, they similarly contrast the phenomenology of perception with the phenomenology of emotion and account for the difference by characterizing emotions as attitudes (2015, 306). Yet Deonna and Teroni do not do enough to highlight what is specific to emotions as attitudes in this further, non-technical sense and how this

---

[26]They approvingly refer to de Sousa (1987, 156f.) who they seem to understand as conceiving of emotions as position-takings. Cf. esp. Deonna and Teroni (2014, 25, n. 21). Cf. also their (2015, 294, n. 1), though here they do not explicitly use the term "position-taking" in connection with de Sousa's view. It seems to me that there is a question how close de Sousa's claim that emotions are attitudes is to the idea of a position-taking. As I understand it, it is principally aimed at capturing the idea that emotions are perspectival in that one cannot hypothetically experience them.

distinguishes them from every form of apprehension.[27] Relatedly, while they note that emotions, but not perceptions, admit of justifying reasons, they do not recognize them as responses to value and hold on to a version of the view that emotions, or their felt aspects in particular, apprehend value (cf. also Sect. 1 in Chapter 2).[28] In this respect, their position conflicts with PT.

My central concern here has been to put the specific sense in which emotional feelings are directed at centre stage and to show how their intentionality and their hedonic dimension jointly give substance to a view that conflicts with an epistemic conception of emotional feeling as apprehending value. While I have focused on AR as the most prominent epistemic conception, my considerations tell against every possible version of the view that emotions or their felt aspects apprehend value. One can read my considerations on directed (dis)pleasure as contributing to the substantive characterization of a general intentional mode exemplified by paradigm emotions; however, if one adopts this reading, this mode is to be conceived as fundamentally different from the type of psychological involvement characteristic of any form of apprehension.

4 Conclusion

In this chapter, I expanded on some of the considerations on emotional feeling I offered in the context of my criticism of AR and showed that these support a very different intentionalist account of emotional feeling. Emotional feeling, as feeling towards, can be understood to make a significant contribution to our psychological lives as a specific form of

---

[27] It is also not clear that the valence of emotions is important to their understanding of them as stances. That said, their proposed explication of the attitudinal character of emotion in terms of felt bodily action readiness is intended to be sensitive to their valence. Cf. (2012, 88). Importantly, in rejecting a hedonic account of valence in favour of a specific pluralistic view, Deonna and Teroni do not understand emotions qua valenced as (dis)approvals along the lines I have proposed. There is more to say about their characterization of emotional feeling in terms felt action readiness by way of a more thorough comparison of their account with PT. However, I here do not take up this issue since, as I argued in Sect. 1 in Chapter 2, their characterization of emotional feeling in terms of felt action readiness faces serious difficulties to begin with.

[28] My own version of the view that emotions are evaluative attitudes is explicitly opposed to the view that they apprehend value. Cf. Müller (2017).

position-taking: in emotional feeling we do not 'take cognizance' of the values of objects; rather we take a (dis)favourable position towards them in response to their value. In the main part of this chapter, I provided a detailed account of the sense in which emotional feelings can literally, rather than just metaphorically, be understood as position-takings. To do so, I first elaborated on the account of the personal dimension of emotional feelings I sketched in Sect. 1.2 in Chapter 2 and argued that emotional (dis)comfort is the felt positive or negative resonance of things with our cares and concerns. I ultimately offered an account of the character of emotional feelings as personal position-takings in terms of the idea that they are ways of finding something (dis)agreeable, where the term "(dis)agreeable" alludes to the felt satisfaction or frustration of the respective cares and concerns. Indeed, in recognizing emotional feelings as stances informed by our complex background of cares and concerns, this picture recognizes them as one of the most subtle and complex form of position-taking we are capable of.

In Chapter 5 of this investigation, I want to look more closely at one specific aspect of the account of emotional feeling that I have explicated in this and the foregoing chapters. One central feature of PT, which crucially distinguishes it from AR, is that it recognizes emotional feelings as being based or grounded on a prior awareness of value rather than being itself disclosive of value. As responses to value, emotional feelings respond to values we are (or seem to be) aware of. I think it important to further expand on this aspect of PT and specify more clearly what this value awareness amounts to. This seems important to me in part by way of offering a complete explication of PT. I thereby also hope to fend off a familiar epistemological objection against value realism that I noted in Sect. 2.2 in Chapter 2, which questions the possibility of a non-mysterious account of the apprehension of value. This should alleviate a concern one might still have with the realist understanding of value implicit in the notion of the formal object of an emotion, as explicated in Sect. 2.2 in Chapter 2 and Sect. 5 in Chapter 3. As I hope to show, there is nothing mysterious about the kind of axiological awareness on which I take emotional feelings to be based.

References

Colombetti, Giovanna. 2005. Appraising valence. *Journal of Consciousness Studies* 12: 103–126.

Dennett, Daniel. 1987. *The intentional stance.* Cambridge, MA: MIT Press.

Deonna, Julien, and Fabrice Teroni. 2012. *The emotions.* London: Routledge.

Deonna, Julien, and Fabrice Teroni. 2014. In what sense are emotions evaluations? In *Emotion and value*, ed. Sabine Roeser and Cain Todd, 15–31. Oxford: Oxford University Press.

Deonna, Julien, and Fabrice Teroni. 2015. Emotions as attitudes. *Dialectica* 69 (3): 293–311.

de Sousa, Ronald. 1987. *The rationality of emotion.* Cambridge, MA: MIT Press.

Düringer, Eva. 2014. *Evaluating emotions.* Basingstoke: Palgrave Macmillan.

Gaus, Gerald F. 1990. *Value and justification.* Cambridge: Cambridge University Press.

Greenspan, Patricia. 1980. A case of mixed feelings: Ambivalence and the logic of emotion. In *Explaining emotions*, ed. Amélie O. Rorty, 223–250. Berkeley: University of California Press.

Helm, Bennett. 2001. *Emotional reason.* Cambridge: Cambridge University Press.

Müller, Jean M. 2017. How (not) to think of emotions as evaluative attitudes. *Dialectica* 71 (2): 281–308.

Müller, Jean M. 2019. Dietrich von Hildebrand. In *Routledge handbook of phenomenology of emotions*, ed. Thomas Szanto and Hilge Landweer. London and New York: Routledge.

Mulligan, Kevin. 2004. Husserl on the "logics" of valuing, values and norms. In *Fenomenologia della ragion pratica*, ed. Beatrice Centi and Gianna Gigliotti, 177–225. Naples: Bibliopolis.

Mulligan, Kevin. 2007. Intentionality, knowledge and formal objects. *Disputatio* 23 (2): 205–228.

Mulligan, Kevin. 2010a. Husserls Herz. In *Husserl und die Philosophie des Geistes*, ed. Manfred Frank and Niels Weidtmann, 209–238. Berlin: Suhrkamp.

Mulligan, Kevin. 2010b. Emotions and values. In *Oxford handbook of the philosophy of emotion*, ed. Peter Goldie, 475–500. Oxford: Oxford University Press.

Mulligan, Kevin. 2013. Acceptance, acknowledgment, affirmation, agreement, assertion, belief, certainty, conviction, denial, judgment, refusal and rejection. In *Judgment and truth in early analytic philosophy and phenomenology*, ed. Mark Textor, 97–136. London: Palgrave Macmillan.

Mulligan, Kevin. 2017. Thrills, orgasms, sadness and hysteria: Austro-German criticisms of William James. In *Thinking about the emotions*, ed. Alix Cohen and Robert Stern, 223–252. Oxford: Oxford University Press.
Mulligan, Kevin, and K. Klaus Scherer. 2012. Toward a working definition of emotion. *Emotion Review* 4 (4): 345–357.
Nussbaum, Martha. 2001. *Upheavals of thought*. Cambridge: Cambridge University Press.
Poellner, Peter. 2016. Phenomenology and the perceptual model of emotion. *Proceedings of the Aristotelian Society* 116 (3): 261–288.
Roberts, Robert C. 2003. *Emotions*. Cambridge: Cambridge University Press.
Sartre, Jean-Paul. 2003. *Being and nothingness*, trans. M.E. Barnes. London and New York: Routledge. Original edition: Sartre, Jean-Paul. 1943. *L'Être et le néant*. Paris: Gallimard.
Scheler, Max. 1973. *Formalism in ethics and non-formal ethics of values*, trans. M.S. Frings and R.L. Funk. Evanston, IL: Northwestern University Press. Original edition: Scheler, Max. 1913–1916. *Der Formalismus in der Ethik und die materiale Wertethik*. Halle: Max Niemeyer.
Schroeder, Timothy. 2007. An unexpected pleasure. *Canadian Journal of Philosophy* 32: 255–272.
Searle, John. 1983. *Intentionality*. Cambridge: Cambridge University Press.
Slaby, Jan. 2008. *Gefühl und Weltbezug*. Paderborn: Mentis.
Teroni, Fabrice. 2007. Emotions and formal objects. *Dialectica* 61 (3): 395–415.
Vendrell Ferran, Íngrid. 2008. *Die Emotionen: Gefühle in der realistischen Phänomenologie*. Berlin: Akademie.
von Hildebrand, Dietrich. 1969. *Die Idee der sittlichen Handlung*. Special Edition. Darmstadt: Wissenschaftliche Buchgesellschaft. Original edition: von Hildebrand, Dietrich. 1916. Die Idee der sittlichen Handlung. *Jahrbuch für Philosophie und phänomenologische Forschung* 3: 126–251.
von Hildebrand, Dietrich. 1953. *Christian ethics*. New York: McKay.
Wollheim, Richard. 1999. *On the emotions*. New Haven and London: Yale University Press.
Zamuner, Edoardo. 2015. Emotions as psychological reactions. *Mind and Language* 30 (1): 22–43.

5

The Evaluative Foundation of Emotional Feeling

Abstract I expand on the position-taking view (PT) by offering an account of the axiological awareness on which emotional feelings are based as responses to value. In doing so, my aim is to elaborate on a central aspect of PT which can seem controversial in light of a common concern about the possibility of value awareness. I initially introduce the view of pre-emotional value awareness which is defended by proponents of PT in the early phenomenological tradition. Rather than adopting their conception of this awareness as a sui generis type of acquaintance with value, I propose that the intuition driving this view can more plausibly be substantiated by thinking of this awareness as a specific form of aspect perception which is based on the concerns of the experiencing subject. This account invokes a familiar type of experience that is widely recognized as a genuine psychological phenomenon. I finally defend this proposal against two objections.

Keywords Awareness of value · Feeling value · Concern-based construal · Concepts · Causal constraint

The position-taking view (PT) recognizes emotional feelings as based on axiological awareness. More specifically, emotional responses to actual exemplifications of their formal object are based on awareness of its exemplification whilst emotional responses to its mere apparent exemplification are based on mere awareness as of its exemplification.

In this last chapter, I would like to shed some more light on the cognitive presuppositions of emotional feelings qua responses to value. My aim in doing so is in part to lay out PT more fully. However, a more detailed account of these presuppositions seems important to me also on additional grounds. In my brief discussion of value realism in Sect. 2.2 in Chapter 2 I noted that some philosophers are sceptical of the possibility of axiological awareness. As they suppose, the only way in which we could have epistemic access to value would be via some mysterious faculty of axiological intuition, a special quasi-perceptual faculty very different from the faculties by means of which we gain awareness of the non-axiological world. (As I noted, the axiological receptivity view (AR) is often put forward as a response to this concern.[1]) What I say in this chapter is also aimed at rebutting this worry. If my considerations are accurate, we can recognize emotional feelings as being based on axiological awareness without any commitment to a mysterious quasi-perceptual faculty. This should also help to further vindicate the realist understanding of formal objects presupposed by ordinary critical practice.

In order to clearly distinguish the value awareness I am concerned with from what I have been calling the cognitive basis of an emotion (cf. Sect. 3 in Chapter 3), I will refer to it as the *evaluative foundation* of emotional feeling. I start by outlining a traditional account of the evaluative foundation of emotional feelings as conceived by several early realist phenomenologists (including centrally von Hildebrand) (Sect. 1). I then go on to elaborate on the core intuition underlying this account and show that we can understand emotional feelings as based on a specific form of aspectual

---

[1] Philosophers concerned to establish the epistemic significance of emotions or emotional feelings sometimes express a more restrictive form of scepticism against axiological awareness. Some of them suppose that occurrent emotion is the only type of experience that plausibly constitutes a non-mysterious form of value apprehension and explicitly oppose views of emotion that assume them to be based on a form of non-emotional value impression. Cf. Teroni (2007, 407). Cf. also Deonna and Teroni (2012, 93f., 103, n. 3).

impression which is structurally on a par with ordinary forms of 'perceiving as', but differs from the latter in that its psychological background comprises our cares and concerns. Taking my inspiration from a specific version of AR, I propose that emotional feelings are based on *concern-based construals* (Sect. 2). In the remainder, this proposal is defended against two objections. The first of these concerns the intellectual capacities required to enjoy concern-based construals (Sect. 3), while the second raises a worry regarding the possibility for them to constitute genuine epistemic contact with value (Sect. 4).

One caveat I ought to add is that I here explicitly choose not to approach the question of the character of the evaluative foundation of emotional feelings by asking whether we enjoy *sense-perceptually based* access to value. This is because a positive answer to this question would only be of limited help in the context of the explicative task I am concerned with. Many emotional feelings are not directed towards objects of sense-perceptual experience, but have their targets supplied by thought, imagination or memory. Yet, these feelings seem to be enjoyed on the basis of genuine value awareness, too. Accordingly, any sense-perceptually based access to value would at best serve as a possible evaluative foundation for certain cases of emotional feeling, but clearly fall short of a form of value awareness that may serve as an evaluative foundation for all of them. In contrast, the account of axiological receptivity I offer in this chapter specifies a type of impression that is general enough to serve as a possible foundation for emotional feelings across the board.

While my account of the evaluative foundation of emotional feeling takes as its starting point the early phenomenological tradition, it is worth noting that the very idea that emotions are based on prior apprehensions as of value has echoes also with traditional versions of psychological appraisal theory (e.g. Arnold 1960; Lazarus 1966).[2] I here refrain from discussing appraisal theory in any detail, though, as my aim is not so much to link my discussion to approaches in empirical psychology as to provide an account of this foundation in line with the manifest image of emotion.

---

[2] These are the two classical formulations of this approach. In the psychological literature, "appraisal" is used to refer to different types of evaluative phenomena, not all of which are cases of apprehending value. However, appraisals are often characterized as ways of detecting the significance of objects and events for their subject.

1 Feeling Value

As PT is commonly elaborated in the early phenomenological tradition, the view comes with a specific understanding of their evaluative foundation. According to Scheler (1973 [1913–1916], esp. 258ff.) and von Hildebrand (1969a [1916], 77ff.; 1969b [1922], 133ff.), emotions are based on a certain type of axiological impression or presentation which goes by the potentially misleading name "feeling value" (*Wertfühlen*). In this context, "feel" does not refer to emotional feeling. Feeling value is a *sui generis* type of acquaintance with value. According to this view, we emotionally feel some way towards a given object in response to axiological properties that are *felt* (or merely apparently felt). Though perhaps initially unorthodox, this view attempts to capture a datum of ordinary experience: often it is *impressions* of value, rather than intellectual value awareness, which engender emotional responses. Thus, one can be afraid of something without knowing or believing that it is dangerous. While, in such cases, there is no intellectual apprehension of disvalue, there is yet a certain impression of danger which motivates one's fear. Often, it is only after one has responded emotionally and enquires into what motivates the response that one intellectually recognizes the situation as dangerous (or, indeed, recognizes that it is not actually dangerous). Similarly, it would seem that someone who is less versed at intellectually monitoring her conduct or determined to uphold a certain idealized self-image and therefore tends not to recognize when an action of hers is degrading can still feel ashamed in response to degrading actions. This person is in some sense acquainted with or 'senses' the degrading character of her action, even though she does not recognize *that it is degrading*.[3] As they elaborate the notion of feeling value, von Hildebrand and Scheler moreover suppose that it includes a perceived demand: in feeling the exemplification of a particular axiological property one also senses a certain solicitation to respond with a particular emotion (cf. Scheler 1973 [1913–1916], 258f.).[4] (The same

---

[3] von Hildebrand (1969a [1916], 80ff.) offers a detailed account of how feeling value differs from recognition and propositional knowledge.
[4] Von Hildebrand does not explicitly think of feeling value as comprising a sensed solicitation. But I take it that, in this point, he follows Scheler, from whom he inherits the basic notion. Cf. also his remarks on the role of motivation in value intuition (von Hildebrand 1969b [1922], 133). This

goes, mutatis mutandis, for merely apparent feelings of value: in this case, one merely apparently senses a certain solicitation to respond emotionally.) The view that we may feel axiological properties and that emotions respond to axiological properties that are felt also surfaces in the more recent debate on emotion in Mulligan's (2004, 216ff.; 2007, 223ff.; 2009; 2010a 232ff.; 2010b, 486f.) work. In contrast to Scheler and von Hildebrand, Mulligan however characterizes this phenomenon primarily as the experience of being 'struck by' value.

Scheler, von Hildebrand and Mulligan seem to me to refer by and large to the same aspect of ordinary experience.[5] While I agree with their main phenomenological intuition, their account of the evaluative foundation of emotional feeling yet strikes me as unsatisfactory in at least two respects. One simply concerns the locutions in terms of which they choose to explicate this intuition. I find the verb "feel" and, likewise, the verb "be struck by" somewhat ill-fitting in this context. The use of "feel" seems unfortunate as it is easily misunderstood as refering to emotional feeling (cf. also von Hildebrand 1969a [1916], 78). "Be struck by" appears unsuitable since it has an obvious implication that considerably restricts the range of impressions to which it applies. Being struck by something seems to entail that one *notices* it. However, as far as ordinary experience is concerned, we may clearly respond with emotional feeling to values we somehow sense but do not yet notice (cf. Müller 2017, 290f.). For example, we often feel fond of people or disdainful towards them in response to specific qualities (e.g. their charm, (in)elegance or (in)sincerity) of which we are aware at some level—they have registered with us—though without having noticed them. We sense their discreet charm and respond with affection but do not realize that they are charming. Similarly, it seems that in order to feel ashamed or guilty for having acted in a way that is incongruent with one's values it is not necessary that one notices the incongruence. Sometimes, it takes time to realize that an action one has performed thwarts one's values.

---

reading is also natural given that he takes values to solicit emotional responses. Cf. von Hildebrand (1953, 38f., 199f., chapter 18) as well as Sect. 5 in Chapter 3, n. 41.

[5] I might add that neither Scheler nor von Hildebrand would fully subscribe to the way in which I understand the formal objects of emotion. Thus, both would maintain that emotions are often responses to species of significance that are not relative to our cares and concerns. Cf. also Sect. 5 in Chapter 3, n. 42. The same goes for Mulligan. I here ignore this difference.

It transpires that one compromised them only by explicitly enquiring into the reasons for one's feeling. Still, even prior to such enquiry, there seems to be a respect in which the incongruence has already been sensed and motivates the way one feels.[6] Note that these concerns do not arise in connection with the verb "sense", which is also sometimes used in this context by the early phenomenologists. This verb is not as readily evocative of emotional feeling and does not entail that the object of awareness is also noticed. In order to characterize the phenomenon in question, I shall therefore use the verb "sense" rather than "feel" or "be struck by".

The second, more important concern with the view offered by Hildebrand, Scheler and Mulligan is that they invoke a sui generis type of awareness. In interpreting ordinary experience in terms of an epistemic contact with value that differs in kind from any type of epistemic contact we enjoy with the non-axiological world they incur a commitment to a special faculty that is tailor-made to provide access to value and thus make their account vulnerable to the familiar concern raised by sceptics about the possibility of value awareness. This strikes me as rather problematic. Instead of specifying the evaluative foundation of emotional feelings to be a sui generis form of value awareness, I take them to be based on value impressions that can be further analysed and shown to form part of a larger, familiar class of impressions. When we feel towards things in response to their significance for us, our awareness of their bearing on our cares and concerns is an instance of the same type of awareness we enjoy of various other types of non-axiological property.

In what follows, I further explain what I take sensing value to amount to. As I propose, emotional feeling is based on a specific type of aspectual impression or *construal* and, as such, on a par with familiar cases of 'perceiving as'. Drawing on Roberts' (2003, 2013) version of AR, I propose that the psychological background or 'set' of this type of impression is constituted by specific cares and concerns. In Roberts' terminology, it is

---

[6]Jane Austen nicely illustrates the difference in question in a passage from *Mansfield Park* when she writes that there "was a charm, perhaps, in [Edmund's] sincerity, his steadiness, his integrity, which Miss Crawford might be able to feel, though not equal to discuss with herself" (2006 [1814], 460). Miss Crawford is clearly not struck by Edmund's charm. She does not notice it. It moreover seems plausible to suppose that she has a certain feeling of fondness for Edmund on this basis without necessarily noticing his charm.

a *concern-based construal* (cf. also Döring 2004, chapters 8 and 9; Slaby 2008, chapter 9, and arguably, Helm 2001, chapter 2).[7]

2 Concern-Based Construals as Receptivity to Value

In order to make emotional feelings intelligible as based on a specific form of aspectual impression, it is necessary to look at aspectual impressions in some more detail. In Sect. 4 in Chapter 3, I specified some central structural features of paradigm cases of aspectual impressions in the context of a brief discussion of familiar cases of 'perceiving as'. As I proposed, 'perceiving as' involves both impressions of certain features or aspects of the object perceived (e.g. the 'duckiness' of the duck-rabbit-figure, a face's similarity to another one) as well as an act of apprehending something against a certain psychological background or 'set' (e.g. a visual image of a duck, an image of another's face). In Roberts' terms, in 'perceiving as', one *construes* a given object in certain terms (supplied e.g. by a particular mental image) and, in doing so, enjoys an impression of a certain feature of that object (a *construal*). With a view to the explanatory task at issue, I want to initially add one important point to this basic account of 'perceiving as'. Intuitively, the impressions that one comes to have in paradigm cases of 'perceiving as' can be cases of coming to be aware of certain features or aspects of the objects perceived. For example, it seems plausible to think that, in construing a face in terms of another one, one can come to register a certain likeness between them. Thus, it is often natural to report this impression as a case of being struck by or noticing a resemblance (cf. Wittgenstein 2010, §113). I would maintain that our registering properties of things in 'perceiving as' need not involve notic-

---

[7] While Roberts, Döring, Slaby and Helm are concerned to illuminate emotion itself, I shall argue that the phenomenon is more appropriately understood as their cognitive foundation. Roberts himself also briefly considers the view that concern-based construals might provide a cognitive foundation of emotion. He rejects this proposal as he supposes that there is no plausible alternative account to be given of emotions themselves once the notion of a concern-based construal is recruited to specify their cognitive presuppositions. Cf. (2003, 139ff.). Roberts does not consider the proposal that they are position-takings.

ing, however. In many cases, e.g. when meeting someone we have not met before, we enjoy an impression of the visual similarity of that person with respect to someone familiar but only come to notice this similarity after a while: in these cases, when one finally notices the similarity, this experience is accompanied by the feeling that it was part of one's background awareness all along, but only has come to be consciously registered now.[8]

In this section, I show that this picture of 'perceiving as' can be significantly generalized. Following Roberts (2003, 2013), I propose that the basic structural features exemplified by familiar cases of sense-experientially based aspectual impressions are exhibited by a much broader class of mental occurrences. There is a large variety of impressions, which are structurally on a par with simple cases of 'perceiving as' in that they involve impressions of features of objects enjoyed by apprehending something in terms of or against a certain psychological background. I begin by describing certain familiar ways in which different types of (broadly speaking) cognitive phenomena may interrelate so as to yield presentations of certain features. I then propose that the characterization I have offered of the evaluative foundation of emotional feelings refers to a construal, too, albeit a construal with a specific background or set provided by our cares and concerns.

Note, to begin with, that the exact same structure displayed by familiar cases of 'perceiving as' is exhibited also by certain types of interplay involving imagination (cf. Roberts 2003, 76f.).[9] For example, it is possible to imagine someone's face in terms of one's current perception of someone else's face so as to enjoy a genuine impression of the former's likeness to the latter. Similarly, one may enjoy impressions of features of objects by imagining them in terms of certain concepts, e.g. by imagining a face in terms of the concepts *rugged* or *kindly*. In these cases, as in ordinary cases of 'perceiving as', one seems to be presented with features of these objects. In each case, the face *appears* a certain way. More-

---

[8]The assumption that 'perceiving as' may be a genuine form of awareness of something is not entirely unproblematic. I take up this idea in some more detail in Sect. 4.

[9]In elucidating the notion of a construal, Roberts mentions a variety of possible interplays between sense-experiences, thoughts, concepts and images. I will here not go through all of the different possibilities he lists and partly choose different examples that, perhaps, somewhat expand the category of construals even beyond the cases Roberts (explicitly) recognizes.

5 The Evaluative Foundation of Emotional Feeling

over, it seems that, like ordinary cases of 'perceiving as', these impressions can constitute cases of registering something about the objects imagined. Thus, in imagining someone's face in terms of one's perception of another face one can come to be aware of a certain likeness between the two faces. Likewise, in imagining a face in terms of the concept *rugged* or *kindly*, one may register an actual feature of the respective face, its ruggedness or kindliness. These examples suggest that the category of construals is broader than the category of 'perceiving as'. They may still seem fairly close to 'perceiving as', however, in that they involve sense-perceptual content. One's primary awareness of the respective object in these cases is still sensory inasmuch as it is supplied by a sensory image. (Moreover, where one construes the imagined object in terms of a sense-perception, this adds an additional sensory dimension to the experience.)

Though this may perhaps initially sound less intuitive, there is reason to suppose that the class of aspectual impressions also comprises occurrences that are entirely non-sensory. Consider, for example, various occurrences which present themselves as a kind of immediate apprehension of non-perceptual similarities. One may be struck by the similarity of someone's character or personality to that of another person. Or consider various experiences one commonly enjoys in purely intellectual contexts. One may be struck by the similarity of Shakespeare's writings to Marlowe's or by the incongruity of the academic style of Harry Frankfurt's essay *On Bullshit* (2005) vis-à-vis the term's normal associations (cf. Roberts 2003, 301). These experiences are entirely non-sensory and yet, on the face of them, presentations of specific features or aspects of something. In having them, something (a person's character, Shakespeare's works, a philosophical article) appears or presents itself in a certain way. Moreover, if one compares them with ordinary cases of 'perceiving as' or imaginatively based aspectual impressions, it seems plausible to suppose that there is a structural kinship also in respect of their dependence on a specific act of construing. One enjoys an impression of the likeness of someone's character to that of another person insofar as one's apprehends the respective attributes and traits of the former against the background of one's grasp of those of the latter. Similarly, one is struck by the incongruence of Frankfurt's analytical approach vis-à-vis his topic in that one apprehends the text in terms of a particular preconception of that topic. Perhaps it is harder in this context to motivate the idea that we enjoy genuine impressions of such non-perceptual similarities or resemblances without noticing them. However, it seems to me that ordinary experience supports this idea: sometimes one notices the likeness of two friends' characters in a particular situation, where this is accompanied by the impression that there has been an appearance or *sense* of similarity all along.[10]

If we consider the variety of mental occurrences that characterize ordinary experience, it seems that in fact a fairly large part of them is comprised by impressions of properties which result from a specific mental interplay in which a given object is apprehended against a certain psychological background. While the basic structure of familiar cases of 'perceiving as' is displayed by all of them, these construals usually involve a more complex interplay, involving several different types of mental occurrence. Indeed, it seems that in ordinary experience, simple cases of 'perceiving as' are rare, or, at least, rarely occur in isolation. For example, when one sees a face and notices its similarity to another one, the impression of similarity one has will usually not be a mere visual one, but rather be informed by a more complex psychological background. This point about the complex psychological background of most ordinary construals is illustrated nicely by the following example from Evelyn Waugh's *Brideshead Revisited*. Considering Waugh's evocative example will at the same time prove helpful in that it allows us to see that sensing value is an instance of the same phenomenon.

On his first visit to Brideshead, the main protagonist of Waugh's novel, Charles Ryder, is collected from the train station by Julia, the sister of his friend Sebastian. In the passage, Waugh describes Charles' first impression of Julia.

> She so much resembled Sebastian that, sitting beside her in the gathering dusk, I was confused by the double illusion of familiarity and strangeness. [...] I knew her and she did not know me. Her dark hair was scarcely longer than Sebastian's, and it blew back from her forehead as his did; her eyes on the darkling road were his, but larger, her painted mouth was less friendly to the world. She wore a bangle of charms on her wrist and in her ears little

---

[10]The example I present below provides further support for this point.

gold rings. Her light coat revealed an inch or two of flowered silk; skirts were short in those days, and her legs, stretched forward to the controls of the car, were spindly, as was also the fashion. Because her sex was the palpable difference between the familiar and the strange, it seemed to fill the space between us, so that I felt her to be especially female as I had felt of no woman before. (1999 [1945], 75)

Charles enjoys a rather complex impression of various (dis)similarities between Julia and her brother. This impression is in part the result of bringing to bear a visual image of Sebastian on his current visual perception of Julia. Julia is apprehended in terms of this image so that she appears (dis)similar to her brother in several respects. His impression is thus a construal. Charles' impression is not confined to visual (dis)similarities, however. Thus, he also has an impression of (dis)similarity in respect of attitude and attributes of character: Julia's mouth appears less friendly. In this respect it seems that the background against which Charles construes her is not limited to a visual image. The way Julia appears to him is informed also by his view or grasp of some of Sebastian's traits or psychological attributes. In fact, Roberts nicely captures the complexity of the background against which Charles construes Julia in writing that Julia's appearance "is invested with Charles' entire friend" (2003, 74). While his construal is (partly) constituted by aspectual impressions along the lines involved in simple cases of 'perceiving as', it is not restricted to these, but further involves impressions of features of Julia which Charles enjoys in virtue of construing her against a much more complex psychological background. In this respect, Waugh's example aptly illustrates the complexity of the kinds of construal that characterize ordinary experience.

If we closely consider Charles' construal of Julia, Waugh's passage can however be seen to help support an additional point. It provides some reason to think that the phenomenon of sensing value can be thought of as a type of construal, too. Note that Charles' experience is describable in part along the same lines I have proposed to characterize the evaluative foundation of emotional feeling: Charles appears to sense a certain familiarity. And here, "familiarity" is not a mere descriptive term; rather, it refers to a type of significance. In having an impression of familiarity, Charles senses a certain significance Julia possesses relative to his *attach-*

ment to Sebastian. Moreover, I would suggest that, insofar as Julia appears familiar, his impression of her can be thought of as comprising also a certain solicitation to feel a particular way towards her—an 'invitation' to take a favourable stand and emotionally 'acknowledge' her as someone familiar. This claim seems to me to make sense of the confusion Charles describes. This confusion is not an intellectual confusion about Julia's identity; it is more plausibly thought of as a confusion about how to feel towards her given a sensed solicitation to acknowledge her as familiar. Now, it does not seem correct to me to think of the impression of familiarity as a further aspect of his experience in addition to the construal. It is rather part of his overall construal of Julia 'in terms of' his friend. In other words, his impression of familiarity, too, can be understood as exhibiting the structural features of common cases of 'perceiving as'. What accounts for Charles' impression of familiarity is that he apprehends Julia in terms of or against the background of his attachment to Sebastian.[11] It, too, is an impression of features of a given object enjoyed in virtue of apprehending it in terms of or against certain psychological background. In contrast to ordinary cases of 'perceiving as', here the background is however provided by a certain concern (his attachment). It is a *concern-based construal.*

As I conceive of the evaluative foundation of emotional feelings, it is a construal of the same type. Thus, my claim that we may sense the significance of things relative to our cares and concerns is not to be understood as positing a kind of sui generis awareness, but rather as referring to a specific type of aspectual impression which we enjoy as a result of apprehending something against the background of our cares and concerns. For you to sense the dangerousness of a given object or event is for you to enjoy an impression of a certain type of relational property as a result of apprehending this object against the background of a certain concern for your well-being or for something else you are attached to: the impression is of a specific (in)congruence of things with concerns in virtue of the fact that the concern serves as the psychological background in terms of which

---

[11] A similar account can be given of his impression of Julia's femininity. Here, "feminine" is not a mere descriptive term, but rather denotes a type of significance. There is also an appearance of sexuality, which directly relates to Charles' sexual interests. This is not to say that he has a sexual desire specifically for Julia; still there is sensed congruence with some concern. Cf. also Roberts (2003, 74).

the object or event is construed. Similarly, for you to sense the degrading character of an action of yours is for you to apprehend this action in terms of certain values. And to sense the goodness of having completed your goals for the day is to enjoy an impression of the congruence of having completed them with your desire to complete them, which is achieved by apprehending your finished work against the background of this desire. These cases of construal are structurally on a par with the way objects are apprehended in terms of a specific psychological background in ordinary cases of 'perceiving as'. Just as we register a certain visual resemblance between two things by letting our awareness of one be informed by a specific mental image or concept of the other, we may also register how things bear on our concerns by having our awareness of the former be informed by the latter.

Although these two kinds of impression are structurally on par, there is at the same time a difference between the way in which features of objects present themselves in concern-based construals and in common cases of 'perceiving as' or other non-axiological construals. Thus, in the case of the former, but not the latter, one's impression also involves a felt solicitation to respond in a particular way: the value property calls for one to feel a particular way. This difference should not be held to speak against concern-based construals being genuine cases of aspectual impression, though. It makes sense to suppose that this felt solicitation is due to the character of the type of property that presents itself in concern-based construals and its intimate connection to our cares and concerns. It is widely held that axiological properties are essentially prescriptive or solicit certain responses. As they are conceived here, the solicitation is grounded in the cares and concerns to which these properties essentially relate. When we apprehend things in terms of our cares and concerns, the relational properties we register have a certain demand character which they owe to the fact that their relata are constituted by those cares and concerns. The (in)congruence of something with your cares calls for a certain response insofar as in caring about the matter you are personally invested in it. In construing something in terms of your cares and concerns, this (in)congruence and the associated demand character become experientially conspicuous.[12]

The account of sensing value that I am offering here is, of course, only a sketch that should provide some initial motivation for thinking that sensing value is structurally on a par with a familiar sort of non-axiological impression. While there is considerable space for further elaboration, I hope that what I have said thus far is enough to show that there is room for alternatives to accounts of sensing value as a sui generis awareness. If this sketch is plausible, there is reason to suppose that we can recognize emotional feelings as responsive to value without incurring any commitment to a special quasi-perceptual faculty. On this alternative proposal, emotional feelings are based on a familiar type of phenomenon, whose instances afford awareness of various different kinds of property—both axiological and non-axiological.

However, it will likely seem that regardless of its initial plausibility my proposed explanation of sensing value requires some further defence. One objection against conceiving of concern-based construals as an evaluative foundation of emotional feeling alleges that this implies a much too demanding requirement concerning the cognitive capacities needed for having emotions. Concern-based construals, it is argued, require the exercise of suitable axiological concepts (i.e. concepts for the respective formal object). It seems that in order to construe something as dangerous, one must possess the concept of danger. Yet, it is plausible that creatures who lack these conceptual capacities are nonetheless capable of emotions (cf. Deigh 1994, 80; Teroni 2007, 407; Deonna and Teroni 2012, 55; 2014, 21 f.). I will respond to this objection in the following section. The remainder of the chapter is then dedicated to what strikes me as a comparatively more serious worry. This worry concerns the assumption I made right at the start regarding the possibility for aspectual impressions to constitute genuine cases of awareness. There are two respects in which one might take issue with this idea. I address them in the final section.

---

[12] I appreciate that there is more to say about how it is that concern-based construals present features of their objects as soliciting particular responses. Though I hope that these remarks suffice to show that this aspect need not be thought to tell against them having the same structural features as ordinary cases of 'perceiving as'.

3   Construals and Conceptual Capacities

There are no doubt cases of construal which involve the exercise of suitable conceptual capacities. For example, in construing a face in terms of the concepts *rugged* or *kindly*, one is deploying these concepts. Here, the impression of ruggedness or kindliness is achieved by exercising concepts for the specific aspect one perceives. Similarly, when one is struck by the incongruence of Frankfurt's analytical approach in *On Bullshit* vis-à-vis his actual topic, one apprehends the text in terms of a particular preconception of this topic. In this case, too, conceptual capacities are clearly involved. This construal is informed by a prior intellectual grasp of the topic and the philosophical approach adopted by Frankfurt, both of which comprise various items of propositional knowledge and belief. These can only be ascribed to someone who is able to exercise the concepts which characterize the relevant propositional contents. While it thus seems hard to dispute that some construals require their subject to be able to exercise suitable conceptual capacities, it is yet a further question whether all construals do. In the literature on 'perceiving as', one finds a familiar line of thought which suggests that the answer to this question is affirmative. It is based on the observation that aspect perceptions are canonically characterized as cases of perceiving something as F, where F stands for the relevant aspect (e.g. the 'duckiness' of Jastrow's figure when it is seen as a duck, the ruggedness of a face when it is perceived as rugged). There is a common assumption that perceiving something as F requires possession and exercise of the concept of F-ness. Though this is less often explicitly stated, one might think that this assumption extends to all aspectual impressions insofar as we can characterize them as cases of construing something as F. (Indeed, many authors use "perceive x as F" more widely to cover also non-sensory aspectual impressions.) Thus, if the axiological impressions I am concerned with are cases of construing something as F (where F stands for the relevant axiological aspect or value), then it can seem that my proposal requires of subjects of emotion that they possess suitable conceptual capacities. More specifically, insofar as concern-based construals are characterizable as construals of x as F (and, in sensory based cases, perceptions of x as F), where F stands for the respective value, it seems to require that subjects of emotion master the corresponding axiological concepts: in order to construe something as dangerous (degrading) one must possess and exercises the concept of danger (of degradation).

In assessing this line of thought, it is important to take into account that the notion of a concept and that of its possession is itself a matter of dispute. According to the common, traditional view, possessing a concept requires several cognitive abilities. Perhaps most centrally, it requires the ability to discriminate things that it applies to from those that it does not apply to. On the traditional view, this is not sufficient, though. As it conceives of the possession of a concept, this moreover involves mastery of its inferential role. That is to say that one must also be sensitive to some of the inferential relations in which contents involving this concept stand to contents involving other concepts and form and revise beliefs in whose content it features in accordance with this inferential role.[13] Less demanding views of concepts require for their possession only the capacity to discriminate things in its extension from those outside it.

Now, plausibly, many non-human animals and infants possess discriminatory capacities that conform to this requirement on concept possession. For example, many non-human animals react differently to situations that are dangerous than to those that are not. In this respect, they might be seen as having a capacity to discriminate between things that fall under the concept of danger and those that do not. Accordingly, if we suppose a less demanding view of concepts, it is not obvious that proponents of the view that emotional feelings are based on concern-based construals need to reject the common assumption that construals require the possession of concepts for the corresponding aspect.[14]

However, the broader consensus in the current debate on intentional mental content as well as in the current Anglophone debate on emotion is that concept possession is to be conceived in more traditional terms (cf. e.g. Tappolet 2000, 179f.; 2016, 17f.; Döring 2004, 249; Deonna and Teroni

---

[13] For example, one should consider revising a belief in whose content the concept features if one has strong reason to doubt the truth of propositions that are entailed by this content. Cf. e.g. Peacocke (1992), Crane (1992), and Brandom (1994, 2000) for accounts of concept possession that stress mastery of the corresponding inferential role. Roberts (1996, 2003) ties possession of a concept to mastery of a language and does not explicitly mention inferential capacities. But I think it is plausible to assume that mastery of a language comes with mastery of the inferential role of the concepts expressed by its terms.

[14] Roberts adopts a move on these lines in his (2009, 221ff.; 2013, 89f.).

2014, 20). Thus, the common assumption about aspectual impressions is more adequately interpreted as invoking more than discriminatory capacities: enjoying a construal of *x* as *F* requires possession and exercise of a concept of *F*-ness, where possession of this concept involves both discriminatory and inferential capacities (cf. also Deonna and Teroni 2014, 21f.). Correspondingly, I will assume that an adequate response to the objection at issue should be based on this interpretation. Accordingly, it is not sufficient to refer to the discriminatory capacities of infants and non-human animals in order to meet this objection. But I think we can give a different response which, as far as I can see, casts doubt on this common assumption also on a more demanding view of concept possession.

The first observation to make in developing this response is that in several paradigm cases of aspectual impressions it seems clearly false to require of its subject that she exercises concepts for the aspect under which the perceived object presents itself. As I have described simple cases of 'perceiving as' (such as seeing an ambiguous figure as a duck/as a rabbit), the cognitive resources that the perceiver brings to bear on her visual experience are specific visual images. On this account, in looking at the duck/rabbit figure one obtains an impression of 'duckiness' by bringing to bear a visual image of a duck on one's visual perception of the figure. This account imposes no requirement on the perceiver's conceptual capacities. Mental images are generally distinguished from concepts. Certainly, they do not count as concepts in the traditional sense. After all, having a visual image does not require sensitivity to any inferential relations. Perhaps authors committed to the standard view of 'perceiving as' are likely to insist that if the impression is really characterizable as a case of seeing the figure *as a duck* then it must impose a constraint on the perceiver's conceptual repertoire. But it is not clear why one should accept this. I take it that what is crucial in this context is whether we can make intelligible how the figure visually appears to the subject—the characteristic impression of the shape of a duck—without invoking the deployment of a corresponding concept. As far as I can see, the proposal that one's sensory awareness of the figure is informed by a visual image can make this perfectly intelligible. In virtue of the specific interplay between the visual image and one's visual awareness of the figure the construal acquires a certain structure or organization. More specifically, the visual image here provides a standard of comparison or congruence relative to which figure can seem (dis)similar or (in)congruent. There is a similarity with the content of this image which is partly underwritten by the arrangement of lines and dots in the figure. For the figure to appear to be duck-shaped is, in effect, for it to appear similar to the content of one's visual image (the shape of a duck). This explains how the figure presents itself to the experiencing subject. Note also that we can likewise explain the switch that occurs when it is seen differently without invoking concepts: this switch occurs when the perceiver brings to bear a different visual image, an image of a rabbit, on her sensory awareness of the figure so that the construal is organized relative to a different standard of comparison. Of course, this is not to rule out that the two impressions can be obtained also by having one's visual awareness of the figure informed by corresponding concepts. Plausibly, they can. But the important point is that this does not seem to be necessary. And this should be enough to challenge the assumption that construing x as F requires possession and exercise of a concept of F-ness.[15]

Now, it might be thought that concern-based construals are considerably more complex than simple cases of 'perceiving as' and that it is therefore not clear that the account I have given of the latter generalizes to the former. Perhaps in the case of concern-based construals, a different type of explanation is needed, which does invoke concepts. It is fair to note in this context that concerns are often, if not typically, mental states with propositional content, such as desires. Hence, since having a concern-based construal presupposes having concerns, this will often require their subject to possess those concepts characterizing the propositional content of the concern on which the construal is based. However, while it is true that many concerns have propositional content, the notion

---

[15] One might, out of deference to philosophical dogma, decide to use the locutions "perceive x as F" and "construe x as F" only for construals where a corresponding concept is being exercised and treat those construals of which this is not true as strongly analogous to, but different, from the former. This is what Roberts (1996, 2003) opts for. I doubt that there is sufficient rationale for doing so given the substantial similarities between both types of impression. To be fair, one may suppose with Roberts that there are certain differences between the impressions depending on whether a concept is exercised. But it is not clear to me that they are significant enough to warrant this restricted usage. I would maintain that there is a clear respect in which in each case the figure appears in the same way or under the same aspect (as Roberts seems to acknowledge). Note also that it is not at all evident that those experiences that have been in the focus of the discussion of 'seeing as' since Wittgenstein's (2010) pioneering discussion involve the exercise of concepts as opposed to visual images.

of a concern is broad enough to include dispositional states which lack such content. Thus, it is broad enough to also include e.g. basic biological aversions to physical harm (cf. also Roberts 1996, 153; 2003, 116, 142). To the extent that concern-based construals may involve such biological concerns, it is thus not clear that they generally display a level complexity that requires the possession of concepts. Note, moreover, that the explanation I have given above of the appearance involved in simpler cases of 'perceiving as' does seem to apply also to the appearances involved in concern-based construals. What accounts for the appearance of value in these cases is a certain type of structure that is imposed on one's primary awareness of their specific object. When the aggressive dog appears dangerous, one's primary visual awareness of the dog is informed by one's concern for physical integrity or safety. This concern likewise serves as a standard of comparison or congruence relative to which the perceived dog can be apprehended as incongruent. The incongruence is underwritten by certain features of which we are aware (e.g. its aggressive look, bared teeth etc.) and which take a certain prominence within one's construal as a result of apprehending the dog in terms of this concern. It is in this way that its potential to harm something that matters to us (our physical well-being) becomes experientially conspicuous. As far as I can see, there is no principled reason why this sort of mental interplay cannot take place in the psychology of non-human animals that are capable of sensory perception and have basic biological concerns. Of course, it is very plausible that human adults are capable of many more and considerably more complex concern-based construals (and, consequently, emotions) than non-human animals and infants (cf. esp. Roberts 2009). Moreover, one may plausibly want to allow that there are certain differences between the character of concern-based construals possessed by humans and the character of those possessed by non-human animals and infants (cf. Roberts 1996, 151ff.; 2003, 115ff.; 2009). And perhaps some of these will have to do with the fact that humans possess concepts, or specifically axiological concepts, understood in the more traditional sense (cf. 2009 as well as n. 15). But it seems to me that the account I have offered provides some ground to suppose that, in principle, concern-based construals are ascribable to creatures that do not share this level of cognitive sophistication.[16] Accordingly, this objection does not seem to me to have much bite against the view of the evaluative foundation of emotional feeling I have suggested.

4 How to Think of Construals as a Form of Epistemic Access

My proposed account of the evaluative foundation of emotional feeling is based on a generalized account of aspectual impressions, which conceives of the these as potentially disclosive of how things are. While I suggested that the claim that aspectual impressions may constitute cases of awareness of features of their objects conforms with ordinary experience and discourse, the proposal may seem in tension with the nature of construals in two respects.

According to one worry one might see with this assumption, there is a tension between the epistemic role I have accorded to aspectual impressions and their essential dependence on a subject's psychological background. One might suppose that, despite being faithful to ordinary discourse and experience, the claim that construals may disclose genuine features of objects conflicts with the fact that it is due to the subject herself, that is, due to the way in which a certain psychological background is brought to bear on her apprehension of a given object, that things appear to her the way they do: How can what manifests itself be part of the way things objectively are if the respective impression is enjoyed because the subject herself 'interprets' them in a specific way by bringing to bear her own psychological background on her awareness of them? If one sees a problem here, one might be inclined to suppose that what shows up in construals is really a property that one has projected into the world—an

---

[16]In a footnote, Deonna and Teroni (2014, 21, n. 8) acknowledge Roberts' (1996, 2003) claim that we can construe things in terms of other representational items than concepts (e.g. images). Yet they insist that, when it comes to axiological construals corresponding axiological concepts must be exercised. I see no reason for treating the axiological case as special. The account I have sketched explains the respective axiological appearance without invoking axiological concepts.

echo of one's own psychology[17]—rather than a feature of its objective layout.

Although it can seem that the dependence of construals on a specific psychological background tells against the epistemic role I accord to them, it is not hard to see that the present concern is misplaced. There is no pressure to think of the features purportedly registered in construals as mere projections if one properly appreciates their nature. Note that what we register in seeing the duck/rabbit figure as a duck is a visual similarity, a resemblance between the figure and what is depicted by a certain visual image (a duck). Likewise, what we detect in apprehending an insult in terms of one's concern to be treated respectfully is a particular incongruence with this concern. The features grasped in both cases are essentially relational.[18] Yet, it is not clear that there is anything problematic about the claim that one registers an actual feature of something by bringing to bear certain aspects of one's psychology on one's awareness of that thing if the feature in question is a (dis)similarity or (in)congruence. In order to register these relational features, one must bring to bear a certain standard of comparison or congruence with respect to which the respective object can be apprehended as (dis)similar or (in)congruent. And this is exactly the role of the psychological background in terms of which the object is construed. The images, concepts, perceptions, thoughts and concerns which may inform one's awareness of a given object in acts of construal supply a standard of comparison or congruence relative to which that object is apprehended as (dis)similar or (in)congruent. If the essentially relational character of the feature registered in these cases is taken into account, the idea that aspectual impressions are the upshot of an act of construing poses no threat to the claim that they may have genuine epistemic import. Rather, their having epistemic import is dependent upon this type of act. Accordingly, there is no conflict between the epistemic role I have accorded to construals and their essential dependence on a subject's psychological background.

---

[17] This metaphor is from Wittgenstein's discussion of 'seeing-as' (2010, §235).
[18] Schroeder (2010, 360) offers a similar defence of the view that 'perceiving as' has epistemic import by stressing the relational character of the features presented.

According to a further, perhaps more severe worry, this role is incompatible with a plausible constraint on epistemic contact. Thus, it is often supposed that for a mental phenomenon to afford epistemic contact with something it must be causally related to it. Yet, it can seem that this constraint precludes construals from affording epistemic contact with the relational features that they appear to make manifest. To explain this worry, I shall first elaborate on the idea of a causal constraint on awareness.

Consider the following passage from Strawson (1974, 71), which illustrates this constraint with respect to perception:

> The concept of perception is too closely linked to that of knowledge for us to tolerate the idea of someone's being in this way merely flukishly right in taking his M-experiences to be the M-*perception* that it seems to be. Only those M-experiences which are in a certain sense dependable are to count as the M-perceptions they seem to be; and dependability in this sense entails dependence, causal or non-logical dependence on appropriate M-facts.

Strawson here proposes that since perception is similar to propositional knowledge in being a form of epistemic contact, visual experiences that count as perceptions must be non-accidentally related to their objects. As he goes on to suggest, this non-accidental connection is to be understood in terms of a certain causal dependence of the experience on its object. The idea that this connection is causal seems to make intelligible its non-accidental character.[19] While Strawson focuses on perception, the proposal he puts forward has also been explicitly defended for the case of propositional knowledge. On Goldman's (1967) view, for any belief to qualify as knowledge it must be caused by the fact that makes it true. On this account, too, it is the non-accidental connection between the state of knowing and its object which makes this idea intuitive. In knowing something to be the case, one's belief that it is the case is not true merely by chance. The idea that it is caused by the relevant fact appears to provide a plausible account of the non-accidental character of this connection.[20]

---

[19] A causal constraint on perception is also endorsed among others by Grice (1961), Goldman (1977), and Huemer (2001).

[20] In this context, Goldman also considers forms of awareness on which propositional knowledge is commonly based, including perception and memory, and proposes that, in these cases, the non-

In light of the thought proposed by Strawson and Goldman it seems compelling to suppose that forms of epistemic contact or awareness of something more generally involve a causal relation between the state of awareness and its object. After all, any form awareness of something involves a non-accidental connection to its object. Generalizing from the case of perception and propositional knowledge, a causal constraint might be thought to make good sense of this link. Accordingly, if construals are to yield awareness of features of their objects, one might think that they, too, are subject to a causal requirement. Yet, it seems that, in this case, the constraint is difficult to satisfy. This is because the relational properties purportedly disclosed by them are not causally efficacious. The visual (dis)similarity between two objects is not a feature apt to cause anything. Likewise, the congruence of a certain fact or state of affairs with one's desire for things to be that way or the incongruence between one's behaviour and one's values are causally inert.[21] While one's *awareness* of these features may be causally efficacious, the features themselves are not. Thus, if one thinks that awareness involves a causal link to its object one might doubt that aspectual impressions can constitute awareness.

While this worry requires somewhat more extensive treatment, it can yet be shown to be unfounded, too. It is certainly uncontroversial that for one's impression of a certain feature to be a genuine case of awareness of that feature it must not merely happen to accord with the way things are. At the same time, the specific account of this connection suggested by Strawson and Goldman is not mandatory. One way to show this is to

---

accidental connection between the state of awareness and its object is likewise underwritten by a causal connection. Cf. (1967, 358ff.).

[21]The same concern is sometimes raised with respect to the possibility of awareness of value more generally, that is, irrespective of the specific understanding of the formal objects of emotions I have here assumed. Cf. McBrayer (2010) on moral 'perceiving as' in this context. (McBrayer's notion of 'perceiving as' differs to a certain extent from the notion of construal I have here elaborated. He does not—or not explicitly—define 'perceiving as' in terms of the specific structure that I take to be essential to it (i.e. apprehending something against a certain psychological background). Also, McBrayer puts 'perceiving as' on a par with 'perceiving that'. I do not wish to commit to this understanding. Accordingly, I do not claim that concern-based construals are ways of being aware *that* that certain axiological facts obtain. What is more, McBrayer invokes a somewhat specific understanding of the causal constraint on awareness, which is perhaps slightly weaker than the most common understanding. Irrespective of these differences, McBrayer's considerations have significantly aided my understanding of the role of causation in connection with axiological awareness and awareness more generally.)

emend the causal constraint they suggest. Another response is to question a general assumption on which the idea of a causal constraint on awareness can be thought to rely. Thus, as I read them, theorists committed to this constraint assume that states of awareness of something have a conjunctive structure in that they are to be analysed as psychological states that are not intrinsically cases of awareness of something but only acquire this status by satisfying additional, extraneous conditions. I personally believe that questioning this assumption is the more appropriate response. However, in order to show that the account of value awareness I favour is compatible with different accounts of awareness, I shall elaborate on both of these responses.

It is possible to emend the causal constraint in a way that allows impressions of (dis)similarities or (in)congruences to be non-accidentally related to the features they are impressions of. For example, while these relational properties are themselves causally inert, one might think that they supervene on features that have causal powers.[22] On this view, the visual similarity between two objects supervenes on certain perceptible features of them, which are apt to cause perceptual experiences (e.g. the specific lines and dots on the drawing constitutive of the duck/rabbit-figure). Likewise, one might argue, when you act in violation of your values, the respective (in)congruence is supervenient on certain non-axiological properties of your action, including its goal or aim, the reasons for which you performed it etc., which are themselves causally efficacious. If this is correct,

---

[22]The response I develop here is based on McBrayer's (2010, 302f.) response to the charge that moral 'perceiving as' requires a causal constraint. McBrayer's considerations may be seen to also point towards alternative responses in connection with different metaphysical views of the nature of concern (in)congruence. For example, a different kind of response might be given on the basis of the view that (in)congruence with our concerns is a higher-level natural property, which is reducible to lower-level natural properties that are themselves causally efficacious. Cf. (ibid., 297ff.). The specific response on which I focus in the main text is based on a comparatively weaker metaphysical view regarding the link between formal objects and non-axiological properties, on which they supervene on non-axiological properties. I believe that many philosophers would be sympathetic to this view. Some might instead opt for a particularist understanding of this connection. Cf. Dancy (1993) for the particularist case against the supervenience of the axiological on the non-axiological. Particularists recognize axiological properties as being grounded in or 'resultant from' non-axiological properties. This link might be seen as being itself sufficiently robust to vindicate the epistemic import of concern-based construals. As Dancy (ibid., 74) elucidates the concept of resultance, he likens the relation to that of token identity. Note that if it is correct that concern (in)congruence is token identical to a certain arrangement of non-axiological features, which are themselves causally efficacious, it seems that the causal constraint on axiological awareness is met.

5 The Evaluative Foundation of Emotional Feeling

there is room to make sense of a non-accidental connection between the respective construal and the relational property in question on the basis of the assumption that it is the subvenient properties that cause this construal. It is not accidental for you to enjoy an impression of your action being incongruent with your concerns when the impression is caused by features of your action on which its incongruence with those concerns supervenes. This is because whenever an action of yours exemplifies these features, it will be incongruent with those concerns.[23]

These considerations suggest that the lack of a causal connection between the features I take to be disclosed by an aspectual impression and the construal itself does not entail that the impression is only accidentally related to these features. In order to make sense of a certain impression as non-accidentally related to the feature it makes manifest, we do not need to posit a causal link between them. Rather, we can make sense of this relation by appealing to a causal connection to other properties that bear a suitably intimate relation to this feature. In this respect, the worry that construals may not disclose (dis)similarities or (in)congruences since these relational properties are causally inefficacious seems misplaced.

There is yet a further way to make construals intelligible as potentially disclosive of relational properties whilst acknowledging that the respective impression must be non-accidentally related to them. As noted above, the idea of a causal constraint on epistemic contact can be seen as based on a specific assumption. According to this assumption, we should think of awareness of something as a mental state that is not intrinsically a case of epistemic contact (such as a visual experience *as of* something or a belief),

---

[23] McBrayer (2010, 304) describes a scenario that can seem to pose a problem for a defence of the possibility of axiological awareness along these lines. He does not set up the case in terms of the view of axiological properties I am assuming, but the scenario can be reformulated accordingly. In some cases, a certain action may be incongruent with one's concerns in virtue of certain non-axiological or natural facts of which one is aware but would still be incongruent with them in virtue of some other feature of which one is not aware if the facts were different. In such a case, one might suppose, the counter-factual dependence between the non-axiological and the axiological is insufficiently tight for the proposal to work. The problem is, as McBrayer suggests that, "the [axiological] facts do not seem to be suitably sensitive to the natural facts of which the subject is aware" (ibid., 304).

I must admit that I am not sure I fully understand the challenge. Maybe there is an inclination here to deny that the subject enjoys awareness of the incongruence. But I am not sure I share this intuition. In this respect, I am inclined to agree with McBrayer when he suggests as one possible response (among others) is that one might question that the sensitivity at issue is a necessary condition for axiological awareness. Cf. (ibid., 305).

but think of this status as conferred on it in virtue of satisfying further, non-psychological conditions. This is a substantive assumption which is ultimately based on the familiar *argument from illusion*.[24] A different way of answering the objection is thus to reject this assumption and to instead opt for a view on which construals can intrinsically be a form of epistemic contact.

To get clear on what is at issue, let me illustrate the argument from illusion for the specific case of construals. We can think of it as purporting to show that construals cannot intrinsically or by their very nature afford epistemic contact since it is possible to *mis*construe a given object so as to enjoy an illusory impression of (dis)similarity or (in)congruence. The argument starts from the observation that veridical impressions of (dis)similarity or (in)congruence, which constitute awareness of these features, and non-veridical impressions as of (dis)similarity or (in)congruence are subjectively indiscriminable. For any veridical impression of (dis)similarity or (in)congruence there is also a corresponding illusion, which merely seems to disclose a relational property and cannot be told apart from the former on phenomenological grounds. It then proceeds on the basis of a further assumption regarding the link between the subjective indiscriminability of experiences and the way they are metaphysically related. According to this assumption, for awareness-constituting impressions of (dis)similarity or (in)congruence and corresponding illusions to be subjectively indiscriminable is for the former to be 'just like' the latter and thus for both to ultimately constitute same kind of mental occurrence. The final step assimilates the former to the latter: Since illusory cases are obviously not intrinsically disclosive, it is supposed that awareness-constituting impressions are neither. Both are intrinsically only seeming cases of awareness of relational properties.

To accept this line of thought is to deny that construals can ever by their very nature be genuine cases of registering aspects and thus *relations*

---

[24] For a very clear account and criticism of this argument in its various different guises, cf. Dancy (1995). Dancy makes a compelling case for the claim that reductive accounts of propositional knowledge rely on a version of the argument form illusion, too.

to the way things are.[25] When they are disclosive of (dis)similarities or (in)congruences, this is extraneous to their psychological nature, which is exhaustively characterized in terms of them being experiences *as of* such properties. Accordingly, there is then a substantial task to specify additional constraints whose satisfaction makes construals a case of epistemic contact with (dis)similarity or (in)congruence: one needs to specify a connection between them and exemplifications of these properties which accounts for the intuition that awareness-constituting impressions non-accidentally accord with how things are. More precisely, construals that constitute awareness of relational features are now conceived as having a conjunctive structure consisting of (i) an impression which, by its nature, is no more than a seeming awareness of a relational feature, but which (ii) is also in accordance with reality and (iii) moreover fulfils some further condition that renders it non-accidentally veridical. The causal connection invoked by Strawson and Goldman can be understood as a candidate for this further condition.

Importantly, however, the argument from illusion does not force one to assume that construals that constitute awareness of (dis)similarity and those that are mere impressions as of similarity are the same kind of mental occurrence. This is because the subjective indiscriminability of two experiences does not provide a sufficient reason to draw this metaphysical conclusion. While it may provide *a* reason to suppose this, it is far from clear that this conclusion is mandatory. Accordingly, this argument leaves open the possibility to defend a disjunctive account of construals by resisting the inference from subjective indiscriminability to sameness in kind. According to such an account, aspectual impressions or construals come in two different kinds. One kind is such that the impressions we enjoy in virtue of apprehending things against a certain background are cases of awareness of relational features of them; the other kind is such that it merely seems to us as though they are. If we opt for this type of picture, there is no need to offer a substantive account of non-psychological conditions whose satisfaction allows for awareness-constituting construals to be non-accidentally related to the features they disclose. Instead, the

---

[25] It is worth noting that Roberts himself (implicitly) denies this. As he claims, in construals properties are perceived in a non-factive sense of the term. Cf. (2013, 40). Roberts opts for this account explicitly in order to make room for cases of misconstrual.

intuitive difference between impressions that constitute awareness of relational properties and impressions as of them that are merely accidentally in accord with the world is captured simply insofar as the former, but not the latter, are intrinsically disclosive of such properties.

I believe that the right response to the worry we have been considering is precisely to question the conjunctive picture of awareness on which it can ultimately be seen to rely. If we reject this picture and opt for a disjunctive view of construals the issue of whether construals can be caused by the features I take them to disclose no longer matters for their intelligibility as possible cases of epistemic contact with them. This question only arises once we assume that construals cannot be intrinsically disclosive of (dis)similarities or (in)congruences. That said, I appreciate that not everyone will be happy to accept a disjunctive view of construals. Disjunctivism is, admittedly, a minority position and there are several further issues which would need careful discussion by way of further elaboration and defence (cf. e.g. Haddock and MacPherson 2008; Willaschek 2013). It is not my purpose here to enter this discussion. The remarks I have offered should be sufficient, however, to show that the worry at hand relies on a contestable overall picture of awareness. Moreover, the first response I have sketched to this worry should be sufficient for those sympathetic to a conjunctive view of awareness to recognize construals as potentially disclosive of relational properties, too.

5 Conclusion

My aim in this chapter has been to supplement my main exposition of PT by clarifying the character of the evaluative foundation on which emotional feelings depend qua responses to value. I proposed that this foundation is a specific kind of non-intellectual axiological awareness which is constituted by a specific form of aspectual impression based on our cares and concerns. Although being congenial to the intuition underlying the account of this foundation offered by Scheler, von Hildebrand and Mulligan, the view I have offered differs crucially from their account. Rather than constituting a sui generis form of epistemic access, the evaluative foundation of emotional feeling is a specific instance of a familiar type of phenomenon, which is ubiquitous in ordinary experience and provides epistemic access to other kinds of (non-axiological) relational property. Accordingly, the view offers a non-mysterious epistemology of value and thus shows a familiar objection to the possibility of axiological awareness to be unfounded. It thereby rebuts one remaining concern one might have with the commitment to axiological realism implicit in our ordinary assessments of emotions as fitting: there is no reason to be sceptical about the existence of properties such as danger or offensiveness on the grounds that no plausible epistemology of them can be given. We can make good sense of our awareness of them if we suppose that formal objects essentially consist in the bearing of things on our cares and concerns and understand the respective axiological awareness to take the form of a specific type of aspectual impression in which things are apprehended against the background of those cares and concerns.

References

Arnold, Magda. 1960. *Emotion and personality*, vol. 1. New York: Columbia University Press.
Austen, Jane. 2006. Mansfield Park. In *The complete novels*. London: Penguin (Original edition 1814).
Brandom, Robert. 1994. *Making it explicit*. Cambridge, MA: MIT Press.
Brandom, Robert. 2000. *Articulating reasons*. Cambridge, MA: MIT Press.
Crane, Tim. 1992. The nonconceptual content of experience. In *The contents of experience*, ed. Tim Crane, 136–157. Cambridge: Cambridge University Press.
Dancy, Jonathan. 1993. *Moral reasons*. Oxford: Blackwell.
Dancy, Jonathan. 1995. Arguments from illusion. *The Philosophical Quarterly* 45 (181): 421–438.
Deigh, John. 1994. Cognitivism in the theory of emotion. *Ethics* 104: 824–854.
Deonna, Julien, and Fabrice Teroni. 2012. *The emotions*. London: Routledge.
Deonna, Julien, and Fabrice Teroni. 2014. In what sense are emotions evaluations? In *Emotion and value*, ed. Sabine Roeser and Cain Todd, 15–31. Oxford: Oxford University Press.
Döring, Sabine. 2004. *Gründe und Gefühle*. Habilitationsschrift [Second Book]. Duisburg-Essen University.

Frankfurt, Harry. 2005. *On bullshit*. Princeton: Princeton University Press.
Goldman, Alvin. 1967. A causal theory of knowledge. *The Journal of Philosophy* 64 (12): 357–372.
Goldman, Alvin. 1977. Perceptual objects. *Synthese* 35 (3): 257–284.
Grice, H. Paul. 1961. The causal theory of perception. *Proceedings of the Aristotelian Society, Supplementary* 35: 121–152.
Haddock, Adrian, and Fiona MacPherson (eds.). 2008. *Disjunctivism*. Oxford: Oxford University Press.
Helm, Bennett. 2001. *Emotional reason*. Cambridge: Cambridge University Press.
Huemer, Michael. 2001. *Scepticism and the veil of perception*. Lanham: Rowman & Littlefield.
Lazarus, Richard. 1966. *Psychological stress and the coping process*. New York: McGraw-Hill.
McBrayer, Justin P. 2010. Moral perception and the causal objection. *Ratio* 23 (3): 291–307.
Müller, Jean M. 2017. How (not) to think of emotions as evaluative attitudes. *Dialectica* 71 (2): 281–308.
Mulligan, Kevin. 2004. Husserl on the „logics" of valuing, values and norms. In *Fenomenologia della ragion pratica*, ed. Beatrice Centi and Gianna Gigliotti, 177–225. Naples: Bibliopolis.
Mulligan, Kevin. 2007. Intentionality, knowledge and formal objects. *Disputatio* 23 (2): 205–228.
Mulligan, Kevin. 2009. On being struck by value. In *Leben mit Gefühlen*, ed. Barbara Merker, 141–161. Paderborn: Mentis.
Mulligan, Kevin. 2010a. Husserls Herz. In *Husserl und die Philosophie des Geistes*, ed. Manfred Frank and Niels Weidtmann, 209–238. Berlin: Suhrkamp.
Mulligan, Kevin. 2010b. Emotions and values. In *Oxford handbook of the philosophy of emotion*, ed. Peter Goldie, 475–500. Oxford: Oxford University Press.
Peacocke, Christopher. 1992. *A study of concepts*. Cambridge, MA: MIT Press.
Roberts, Robert C. 1996. Propositions and animal emotion. *Philosophy* 71: 147–156.
Roberts, Robert C. 2003. *Emotions*. Cambridge: Cambridge University Press.
Roberts, Robert C. 2009. The sophistication of non-human emotions. In *Philosophy of animal minds*, ed. Robert W. Lurz, 218–236. Cambridge: Cambridge University Press.
Roberts, Robert C. 2013. *Emotions in the moral life*. Cambridge: Cambridge University Press.

Scheler, Max. 1973. *Formalism in ethics and non-formal ethics of values*, trans. M.S. Frings and R.L. Funk. Evanston, IL: Northwestern University Press. Original edition: Scheler, Max. 1913–1916. *Der Formalismus in der Ethik und die materiale Wertethik*. Halle: Max Niemeyer.

Schroeder, Severin. 2010. A tale of two problems: Wittgenstein's discussion of aspect perception. In *Mind, method and morality*, ed. John Cottingham and Peter Hacker, 352–371. New York: Oxford University Press.

Slaby, Jan. 2008. *Gefühl und Weltbezug*. Paderborn: Mentis.

Strawson, Peter F. 1974. Causation in perception. In *Freedom and resentment and other essays*, ed. Peter F. Strawson, 76–89. London: Methuen.

Tappolet, Christine. 2000. *Émotions et valeurs*. Paris: Presses Universitaires France.

Tappolet, Christine. 2016. *Emotions, values and agency*. Oxford: Oxford University Press.

Teroni, Fabrice. 2007. Emotions and formal objects. *Dialectica* 61 (3): 395–415.

von Hildebrand, Dietrich. 1953. *Christian ethics*. New York: McKay.

von Hildebrand, Dietrich. 1969a. *Die Idee der sittlichen Handlung*, Special Edition. Darmstadt: Wissenschaftliche Buchgesellschaft. Original publication: von Hildebrand, Dietrich. 1916. Die Idee der sittlichen Handlung. *Jahrbuch für Philosophie und phänomenologische Forschung* 3: 126–251.

von Hildebrand, Dietrich. 1969b. *Sittlichkeit und ethische Werterkenntnis*, Special Edition. Darmstadt: Wissenschaftliche Buchgesellschaft. Original publication: von Hildebrand, Dietrich. 1922. Sittlichkeit und ethische Werterkenntnis. *Jahrbuch für Philosophie und phänomenologische Forschung* 5: 463–602.

Waugh, Evelyn. 1999. *Brideshead revisited*. New York: Back Bay Books (Original edition 1945).

Willaschek, Marcus (ed.). 2013. *Disjunctive accounts in epistemology and in the philosophy of perception*. London: Routledge.

Wittgenstein, Ludwig. 2010. *Philosophical investigations*, ed. Peter Hacker and Joachim Schulte, trans. G.E.M. Anscombe, P. Hacker, and J. Schulte, 4th ed. Oxford: Blackwell. Original edition: Wittgenstein, Ludwig. 1953. *Philosophische Untersuchungen* [Philosophical Investigations], trans. G.E.M. Anscombe. Oxford: Blackwell.

6

Conclusion

Abstract This chapter provides a concise summary of the main arguments and conclusions of this book. The upshot of my critique of the dominant intentionalist view (AR) and my positive contribution towards a more adequate alternative (PT) are laid out.

Keywords Emotional feeling · Axiological receptivity · Position-taking

Without the characteristic sense of being affected that is essential to occurrences of fear, anger, pride and admiration our psychological lives would be significantly impoverished. Emotions make a distinctive contribution to our psychological lives *qua feeling*. The pre-theoretical importance of emotion, it seems, is largely due to their affective character.

In this investigation, I have been concerned with a currently prominent view of what makes emotional feelings important. Many philosophers in the more recent debate on emotion believe that emotional feelings matter inasmuch as they constitute a specific form of *psychological involvement with the world*. According to intentionalism about emotional feeling, our sense of being affected in emotion is significant inasmuch as it is a specific mode of intentionality.

My discussion was based on the assumption that this view articulates an important intuition. At the same time, it was driven by the conviction that most of its proponents drastically mischaracterize the intentional features of emotional feelings and, accordingly, their place in our mental lives. There is a strong tendency to suppose that the felt dimension of emotion is *epistemically* significant. According to the view that emotional feeling is receptivity to value (AR), its role is to *acquaint us with* the significance of things in our environment—in feeling afraid or angry we 'take cognizance' of the value of a certain object or event. My central concern in this book has been to show that this view significantly distorts the manifest image of emotion and to offer and substantiate a view that is more faithful to our ordinary conception of emotional feelings and their significance.

As I argued, our ordinary conception of emotion does not represent the felt inner agitation of emotion as an impression or presentation, but as *feeling towards*. In occurrent emotion, we feel good or bad towards an object or event. This feeling is *directed* or *aimed* towards that object or event, rather than being a case of receptivity. To characterize emotional feelings as intentional in this way is, in part, to think of them as *responses* to some aspect of this object or event, including, most importantly, the corresponding formal object. In this respect, they essentially differ from impressions or presentations. Moreover, as responses to their formal objects, they *presuppose* awareness of their formal objects rather than providing such awareness.

While this explication of our ordinary conception of emotional feelings is in sharp conflict with AR, I suggested that it simultaneously supports an alternative account of their significance. In line with a popular early realist phenomenological view of emotion, I proposed that the felt agitation of emotion is a *position-taking* (PT). Feeling afraid, angry, proud or remorseful is not a matter of 'taking cognizance' of the value of some object or event; it is rather about what we 'make of' this object or event in light of its value—about our position towards it. Inasmuch as we feel good or bad about something because of its value, we adopt a (dis)favourable stand towards it in response to its value. In this respect, my proposed explication of the manifest image of emotion supports a view of emotional feelings as making a contribution to our mental lives that is, in a certain sense, the exact opposite of the psychological role accorded to them by AR.

My detailed elaboration of the view that emotional feelings are position-takings can be seen to constitute the main positive contribution of this investigation to an adequate intentionalist understanding of emotional feeling. While several authors in the early realist phenomenological tradition as well as a few contemporary theorists recognize emotional feelings as takings of a (dis)favourable stand, they do not say enough by way of elucidating the idea of an affective position-taking. However, this seems important if we are to understand PT as expressing a substantial claim about emotional feeling and thus to properly appreciate its place in our psychological lives. I elaborated PT by arguing that the hedonic character of emotional feelings relates to our cares and concerns. The way we feel in having an emotion (good/bad) is to be understood in terms of the felt frustration or satisfaction of particular concerns: we feel good or bad insofar as we feel satisfied or frustrated qua subject of those concerns. This makes emotional feelings intelligible as a form of (dis) approval: insofar as the way we feel towards something is directed at that thing, we thereby find it *(dis)agreeable*, where the respective '(dis)agreement' is the felt satisfaction or frustration of specific concerns. This intimate connection between the character of emotional feelings as ways of being personally affected and their character as a specific kind of stance we adopt towards the world seems to me to articulate a crucial aspect of what is pre-theoretically important about them.

While giving a more substantial account of the character of emotional feeling as position-takings seemed most central to show that PT is a serious alternative to AR, I moreover explicated the view in one additional respect. As responses to value emotional feelings are based on axiological awareness. My final considerations were supposed to show how we can account for this awareness without invoking any problematic commitment to a special, sui generis form of epistemic contact with value. While sympathetic to the early realist phenomenological conception of this foundation as a form axiological receptivity, I argued that it need not be thought of as a sui generis form of epistemic contact. Rather, emotional feelings are based on a specific type of axiological aspectual impression or *construal*: we register the significance of something relative to our concerns by apprehending it against the background of those concerns in a manner structurally analogous to our grasp of visual (dis)similarities in ordinary cases of 'perceiving-as'. I thus offered an account of our epistemic access to the formal objects of emotions, according to which this access is a specific case of a familiar type of phenomenon.

Some of my discussion will perhaps have seemed unusual given its extensive preoccupation with specific subtleties concerning the way emotional feelings feature in ordinary experience and discourse. It may at first sight seem slightly excessive to spend several sections detailing the precise sense in which a certain psychological occurrence is directed towards something. However, as I hope is sufficiently clear by now, this investigation was not motivated by a mere interest in phenomenological niceties. Whether or not we appreciate subtleties of this kind has important consequences for our understanding of the specific contribution made by emotional feelings to our mental lives. Indeed, as the case of AR demonstrates, insensitivity to them may lead to a seriously distorted conception of their psychological role. Emotional feelings are important not in that they teach us about the significance of things; rather, they constitute a distinctive kind of *response* to their significance. This response is crucially shaped by their personal character: in being affected by something, it is *us*—as subjects with certain cares and concerns—who take a stand on it.

Index

A

action tendency 23, 26, 35, 109
affect 2, 3, 5, 6, 9, 18–20, 23, 25, 45, 55, 57, 58, 75, 76, 82, 94, 98, 100, 145. *See also* being affected; emotional feeling; *Gemütsbewegung*; stirring of the sensitive mind
Alvarez, M. 64
Ammann, C. 6
apprehension 6, 7, 33, 39, 41, 53, 56, 59, 62, 68, 71, 79, 80, 91, 103, 104, 108, 109, 119–125, 127, 132, 133, 138, 139, 141. *See also* cognizance-taking
   of value 8, 12, 23, 24, 52, 56, 68, 72–74, 79, 80, 94, 100, 103, 109, 110, 114–117, 131, 133. *See also* axiological receptivity; feeling, of value; impression, of value; perception, of value; presentation, of value; value/disvalue, receptivity to
approval/disapproval 94–96, 100, 105–107, 109, 147. *See also* attitude, pro-/con-; favour/disfavour
argument from illusion 138, 139
Arnold, M. 23, 115
assent 9, 56, 74, 98, 100
attitude 8, 30, 108, 123
   evaluative 107, 109
   pro-/con- 93, 94, 96. *See also* approval/disapproval; favour/disfavour
Austen, J. 118
awareness 20, 28, 68, 77, 99, 103, 104, 114, 118–121, 125, 126, 129, 131–135, 137–140, 147. *See also* apprehension

causal constraint on 134–136.
See also perception, causal
constraint on
of value 6, 12, 26, 52, 57, 60, 72,
73, 93, 110, 114–118, 124,
126, 135–137, 140, 146
axiological realism 11, 12, 18, 41–43,
45, 114, 141
emotions, formal object of 42
axiological receptivity (AR) 46,
57, 77. See also feeling, of
value; impression, of value;
perception, of value; presentation, of value; value/disvalue,
receptivity to

B
Bain, D. 35
Bedford, E. 3
being affected 18–21, 25, 27, 32, 52,
55, 57, 75, 76, 81, 84, 98, 99,
101, 145–148. See also affect;
emotion, felt aspect of; emotional feeling; *Gemütsbewegung*;
stirring of the sensitive mind
Bittner, R. 63, 64
Brady, M. 6, 7, 53, 65
Brandom, R. 128
Broad, C.D. 27

C
Calhoun, C. 4
Cannon, W. 22
Castelfranchi, C. 27
Charland, L. 34
Chudnoff, E. 56
Cobos, P. 22

cognizance-taking 5, 8, 83, 90, 146.
See also apprehension
Colombetti, G. 92
concept 71, 120, 125–127, 129, 130,
132, 133
possession of 126–129, 131
concern 4, 8, 12, 25, 27, 28, 30,
32–34, 41, 45, 80–82, 90, 99,
102, 104–106, 110, 115, 117,
118, 120, 124, 130, 140, 148
congruence/incongruence with
26, 30, 33, 41, 43, 44, 79–82,
99, 102, 103, 107, 117, 118,
124, 126, 131, 133, 136, 137,
141, 148
satisfaction/frustration of 33,
101–106, 110, 147
construal 25, 77, 119–123, 127,
129, 130, 132–135, 137–140.
See also impression, aspectual;
perception, 'perceiving-as';
presentation, aspectual
concern-based construal 105, 115,
119, 120, 124–128, 130, 132,
135, 136, 147
Cova, F. 19
Crane, T. 128
Cuneo, T. 6

D
Damasio, A. 22, 28
Dancy, J. 136, 138
Deigh, J. 126
Dennett, D. 97
Deonna, J. 3, 6, 9, 12, 19, 21, 23, 29,
31, 53, 58, 60, 62, 65, 68, 71,
73, 95–97, 99, 100, 102, 104,
107–109, 114, 126, 128, 132

Descartes, R. 24
de Sousa, R. 39, 70, 79, 108
Dietz, C. 53, 63, 65, 67
direction of fit 97
   mind-to-world 96
   world-to-mind 96
disjunctivism 73, 99, 139, 140
Dokic, J. 6, 46, 56
Donnellan, K. 67
Döring, S. 3, 6, 42, 43, 46, 77, 119, 128
Düringer, E. 43, 102

E

Ekman, P. 32
emotion 69
   attitudinal view of 23, 107–109. *See also* attitude, evaluative
   cognitive basis of 68, 69, 75, 114
   comfort/discomfort of 11, 12, 27–32, 34, 36, 45, 61, 91, 105, 106, 110. *See also* concern, satisfaction/frustration of; emotion, hedonic tone of; emotion, pleasure/displeasure of; emotion, valence of
   compound view of 4, 83, 84
   felt aspect of 2, 4, 6, 10–12, 18, 29, 45, 55, 64, 66, 67, 72, 74, 76, 84, 90, 93, 96, 99, 101, 107–109, 146. *See also* affect; being affected; emotional feeling; *Gemütsbewegung*; stirring of the sensitive mind
   formal object of 11, 12, 18, 36–46, 52, 69–71, 73, 74, 78, 79, 81, 90, 98, 99, 107, 108, 110, 114, 117, 126, 135, 136, 141, 146, 148. *See also* concern, congruence/incongruence with
   hedonic tone of 11, 25, 28–36, 45, 55, 90, 92, 94, 95, 100–105, 109, 147. *See also* concern, satisfaction/frustration of; emotion, comfort/discomfort of; emotion, pleasure/displeasure of; emotion, valence of
   intelligibility of 11, 39, 44, 67, 70, 71, 78, 79, 82, 94
   judgmentalism about 9, 97, 99, 100. *See also* judgment, evaluative
   pleasure/displeasure of 25, 27–36, 55, 59, 75, 91–95, 101–105, 147. *See also* concern, satisfaction/frustration of; emotion, comfort/discomfort of; emotion, hedonic tone of; emotion, valence of
   target of 4, 30, 33, 36, 59, 61, 63, 64, 67–73, 99, 100, 115
   valence of 29, 30, 53, 92–95, 109. *See also* concern, satisfaction/frustration of; emotion, comfort/discomfort of; emotion, hedonic tone of; emotion, pleasure/displeasure of
emotional feeling 3–6, 8–11, 13, 17–32, 34–36, 45, 52, 54–60, 62–71, 73–76, 78–84, 90–93, 96, 98–101, 103–107, 109, 110, 113, 114, 118, 119, 126, 128, 145–148. *See also* affect; being affected; emotion, felt aspect of; *Gemütsbewegung*; stirring of the sensitive mind

axiological receptivity view of 6–9, 11, 12, 39, 42, 44–46, 52–58, 60, 63, 65, 69, 71, 73, 74, 76, 82, 83, 90, 91, 93, 95, 97, 109, 110, 114, 115, 118, 146–148
  directedness of 8, 12, 53, 59–63, 66–68, 70, 71, 75, 76, 82, 90, 91, 93, 95, 100, 103, 106, 109, 115, 146–148
  evaluative foundation of 8, 12, 72, 114–120, 123, 124, 126, 128, 132, 140. *See also* construal, concern based; feeling, of value
  motivational significance of 35, 36. *See also* action tendency
  position-taking view of 8, 9, 12, 18, 45, 53, 61, 90, 92, 93, 97, 100, 105, 107–110, 114, 116, 140, 146, 147
  towards 12, 52, 53, 59, 64, 72, 78, 82, 90, 92, 96, 104, 107, 109, 110, 116, 124, 146, 147

F
favour/disfavour 59, 90, 92–96, 110, 124, 147. *See also* approval/disapproval; attitude, pro-/con-
feeling 2–5, 7, 10, 19, 22, 25, 26, 35, 92, 94, 104
  Jamesian sensation 20–26, 28, 36, 46
  Jamesian sensations 23
  leibliches Spüren 24, 28
  position-taking view 84
  psychic 24, 28, 29, 31, 32, 101
  towards 6, 12, 52, 53, 58, 60, 63, 82, 83, 90, 104, 105, 146

of value 57, 60, 116–118
felt aspect of 9
Findlay, J.N. 56
Frankfurt, H. 121, 127
Friesen, W.V. 32
Frijda, N. 23

G
Gaus, G. 93
Gemütsbewegung 2, 18, 19, 24, 25, 27. *See also* affect; being affected; emotion, felt aspect of; emotional feeling; stirring of the sensitive mind
Goldie, P. 4, 6, 12, 37, 59, 60, 84
Goldman, A. 134, 135, 139
Gordon, R. 4
Graham, G. 35
Greenspan, P. 27, 94
Grice, H.P. 134

H
Haddock, A. 140
Heidegger, M. 43, 57
Helm, B. 6, 9, 25, 27, 28, 35, 43, 45, 55–58, 73, 74, 76, 100, 119
Hohmann, G.W. 22
Hornsby, J. 63, 73
Huemer, M. 134
Hume, D. 10
Husserl, E. 37, 54–57, 91

I
impression 7, 12, 25, 55, 56, 58, 67, 75–77, 82, 115, 117, 122, 146. *See also* presentation

aspectual 77, 115, 118–127, 129, 132, 133, 135–141, 147. *See also* construal; perception, 'perceiving as'
   of value 6, 7, 9, 42, 52, 54, 56, 58, 74, 114, 116, 118, 123, 124, 127, 130, 137. *See also* axiological receptivity; feeling, of value; perception, of value; value/disvalue, receptivity to
intentionalism 4, 5, 7, 18, 36, 45, 52–54, 82, 83, 90, 97, 109, 145, 147
intentionality 3–7, 9, 10, 12, 13, 30, 34, 35, 37, 38, 52, 53, 58–63, 65–69, 73, 82–84, 91, 93, 96, 99, 102, 107–109, 128, 145, 146. *See also* attitude; apprehension; axiological receptivity; cognizance-taking; direction of fit; emotion, target of; emotional feeling, directedness of; impression; presentation; position-taking (PT); value/disvalue, receptivity to

J
James, H. 2
James, W. 10, 20, 21, 71
Judgment 99
   evaluative 6, 7, 97, 98

K
Kenny, A. 3, 39, 67

L
Lazarus, R. 4, 115
Lemaire, S. 6, 46, 56
Lyons, W. 4

M
Mackie, J.L. 42
MacPherson, F. 140
McBrayer, J.P. 135–137
McDowell, J. 5, 6, 56, 63, 73
Meinong, A. 37, 54, 56, 57
Miceli, M. 27
Müller, J.M. 19, 39, 59, 63, 65, 67–69, 71–74, 76, 77, 79–81, 91, 97, 108, 109, 117
Mulligan, K. 8, 9, 19, 24, 37, 53, 54, 57, 60, 65, 68–70, 73, 75, 79, 91–93, 95, 117, 118, 140

N
Naar, H. 45
Neu, J. 4
Nussbaum, M. 9, 21, 43, 97, 99

P
Peacocke, C. 128
Pelser, A. 6, 65
perception 6, 7, 52, 53, 56, 58–62, 65, 67–69, 73–76, 90, 101, 103, 108, 115, 123, 131, 133–136
   causal constraint on 134
   'perceiving as' 65, 120, 121, 125, 127, 129. *See also* construal; impression, aspectual; presentation, aspectual

of value 7, 42, 46, 55, 68, 69, 73, 77, 114, 115, 126. *See also* axiological receptivity; impression, of value; presentation, of value; value/disvalue, receptivity to
Pfänder, A. 30
Pitcher, G. 3
Poellner, P. 6, 21, 24, 36, 46, 57, 62, 65, 69, 73, 77, 94, 95, 100
position-taking (PT) 5, 8, 9, 12, 53, 59, 83, 84, 90–95, 97–101, 105, 107, 108, 110, 114, 119, 146, 147. *See also* approval/disapproval; attitude, pro-/con-; favour/disfavour
presentation 7, 11, 52, 53, 55, 56, 58–60, 67, 69, 76, 82, 103, 120, 121, 146. *See also* impression
   aspectual 120, 125, 129, 133. *See also* construal; perception, 'perceiving as'
   of value 6, 46, 52, 54, 56, 73, 77, 80, 83, 95, 116, 126. *See also* axiological receptivity; feeling, of value; perception, of value; value/disvalue, receptivity to
Prinz, J. 22, 38, 44
Proust, M. 2

R

reason 63, 73, 76, 78, 82
   explanatory 64, 66
   motivating 58, 63–71, 73–79, 93, 118, 136. *See also* response
   normative 63, 65, 109
Reinach, A. 58
Reisenzein, R. 43

response 12, 52, 53, 59, 62–64, 66–69, 71, 73–81, 92, 95, 97, 99, 125, 146
   to value 8, 9, 12, 44, 46, 69–75, 79–82, 90, 92–95, 100, 102, 103, 105, 107, 109, 110, 114, 116–118, 125, 126, 140, 146–148. *See also* value/disvalue, response
Roberts, R.C. 3, 6, 27, 28, 33, 41, 43, 77, 81, 101, 102, 104, 105, 118–121, 123, 124, 128, 130–132, 139
Rosenthal, D. 25

S

Salice, A. 8, 59
Sartre, J.-P. 57, 77
Scheer, M. 2
Scheler, M. 24, 36, 46, 57, 60, 63, 70, 77, 80, 92, 94, 116–118, 140
Scherer, K. 92
Schroeder, S. 133
Schroeder, T. 27, 28, 32, 33, 102
Searle, J. 96
Slaby, J. 6, 9, 24, 27, 28, 35, 43, 44, 57, 77, 81, 100, 119
Smith, M. 42
stance 8, 97, 108–110, 147. *See also* position-taking (PT)
stirrings of the sensitive mind 2, 11, 18, 19, 24, 55. *See also* affect; being affected; emotion, felt aspect of; emotional feeling; *Gemütsbewegung*
Stocker, M. 24
Strawson, P.F. 134, 135, 139

T

Tappolet, C. 6, 29, 42, 46, 57, 60, 65, 69, 128
Teroni, F. 3, 6, 9, 12, 21, 23, 26, 29, 31, 37, 39, 40, 53, 58, 60, 62, 65, 68, 69, 71, 73, 95–97, 99, 100, 102, 104, 107–109, 114, 126, 128, 132
Thalberg, I. 4

V

value/disvalue
  realism about 13, 42, 110, 114. *See also* axiological realism (AR)
  receptivity to 8, 9, 18, 42, 45, 46, 52, 60, 90, 115, 119, 146, 147. *See also* axiological receptivity; feeling, of value; impression, of value; presentation, of value; perception, of value
  response 8, 9, 12, 70, 73, 74, 79–81, 90, 92–95, 100, 102, 107, 109, 110, 114, 116, 117, 125, 126, 140, 146, 147. *See also* response, to value
  subjectivism about 26, 43, 44, 81
Vendrell Ferran, Í. 24, 28, 30, 56, 57, 70, 93–95
Voigtländer, E. 70
von Hildebrand, Dietrich 8, 9, 19, 37, 44, 53, 57–63, 75, 76, 80, 81, 90–92, 97, 100, 114, 116–118, 140

W

Waugh, E. 122, 123
Weberman, D. 6, 46, 57
Whiting, D. 25, 53, 58
Willaschek, M. 140
Wittgenstein, L. 119, 130, 133
Wollheim, R. 102, 103

Z

Zagzebski, L. 6, 46
Zamuner, E. 36, 67, 71, 95, 107

Printed by Printforce, the Netherlands